Super Easy
Zero Point Weight Loss
Cookbook

100+ Budget-Friendly, Delicious Recipes for Fast and Sustainable Weight Loss Without Counting Calories

Fiona Westbrook

Copyright

Disclaimer

This book is intended for informational and educational purposes only. The recipes, nutritional guidelines, and fitness advice provided are based on the author's research and experience. While every effort has been made to ensure the accuracy and safety of the content, readers are advised to consult with a registered dietitian, nutritionist, or medical professional before starting any new diet or exercise regimen, particularly if they have pre-existing health conditions.

The author and publisher disclaim any liability or responsibility for any adverse effects, loss, or damage caused directly or indirectly by the use or interpretation of the material presented in this book. Individual results may vary, and readers are encouraged to adapt the information to their specific needs.

TABLE OF CONTENT

Introduction

Imagine enjoying a hearty, satisfying meal without a single worry about counting calories or tracking every bite. No more restrictive diets that leave you hungry, drained, and feeling deprived. Just real, delicious food that helps you shed weight effortlessly, while also keeping you energized and fulfilled. Sounds too good to be true? It's not—and you're about to discover how simple and sustainable weight loss can be.

For many of us, the journey toward better health has been marked by frustration and fad diets that over-promise and under-deliver. You might have tried cutting carbs, reducing fat, or obsessively counting every calorie, only to find that such strict regimens are impossible to sustain. Life is busy, and trying to micromanage every meal only adds more stress. Often, the result is falling off the wagon, feeling guilty, and ending up back at square one.

But what if there was a better way? What if you could finally lose weight by eating nourishing, balanced meals that are naturally aligned with your body's needs—without all the math? This book, Super Easy Zero Point Weight Loss Cookbook, was created to offer exactly that: a straightforward, enjoyable approach to weight loss that doesn't feel like a chore.

With this cookbook, you'll discover that weight loss doesn't have to mean giving up the foods you love or spending hours in the kitchen. Instead, this journey is about embracing a lifestyle that feels natural, balanced, and, most importantly, sustainable. Welcome to a fresh, flavorful approach to reaching your health goals—where you can finally enjoy every meal on the path to a healthier you..

Why Zero Point Foods?

Zero-point foods have gained popularity for their versatility and role in weight management. Unlike traditional dieting methods that rely heavily on calorie counting, zero-point foods offer a refreshing approach by focusing on nutritious, whole ingredients that your body naturally processes efficiently. This means you can enjoy meals that keep you full and energized while making it easier to stay on track with your weight loss goals.

Weight loss doesn't need to be an uphill battle, and with the right approach, it can become an enjoyable part of your routine. The zero-point system is flexible enough to adapt to your individual needs and preferences. By focusing on wholesome foods that nourish your body and support weight loss, you're laying the groundwork

1

for lasting changes that go beyond the number on the scale.

Understanding Zero Point Foods

Zero-point foods have transformed the way we approach weight management. By prioritizing nutritious, filling ingredients that naturally support your health, zero-point foods create an eating plan that is flexible, balanced, and easy to maintain. Let's dive into what zero-point foods are, why they're effective, and how they can make your journey to sustainable weight loss easier and more enjoyable.

What Are Zero Point Foods?

Zero-point foods are ingredients assigned no point value within certain weight management programs. They are typically whole, unprocessed foods that are low in calories and rich in nutrients. Unlike traditional diet plans that may require meticulous calorie counting, a zero-point approach emphasizes eating foods that support satiety and nourishment without needing to track every bite.

Common Categories of Zero Point Foods

While the specific list of zero-point foods can vary by program, here are some common categories:

1. Lean Proteins
   - Examples: Skinless chicken breast, turkey, white fish, shrimp, tofu, and eggs.
   - Why They're Zero Point: Lean proteins are low in fat and calories but high in essential amino acids, making them ideal for building muscle and staying full.
2. Fruits
   - Examples: Apples, strawberries, blueberries, oranges, and watermelon.
   - Why They're Zero Point: Fruits contain vitamins, minerals, and fiber. While they have natural sugars, their calorie density is relatively low, making them great for satisfying sweet cravings healthily.
3. Vegetables
   - Examples: Broccoli, spinach, carrots, zucchini, tomatoes, and bell peppers.
   - Why They're Zero Point: Vegetables are nutrient-dense and have a low-calorie count. They provide essential nutrients

like vitamins A, C, and K, along with minerals such as potassium and iron.
4. Legumes and Beans
   o Examples: Black beans, kidney beans, chickpeas, and lentils.
   o Why They're Zero Point: Legumes are rich in fiber and plant-based protein. They help stabilize blood sugar levels and keep you full longer.
5. Low-Fat Dairy and Dairy Alternatives
   o Examples: Fat-free Greek yogurt and unsweetened plant-based milk.
   o Why They're Zero Point: These options are high in protein with minimal calories, providing a creamy texture and rich taste without the excess fat.

These foods form the cornerstone of meals that are satisfying, nutrient-dense, and conducive to weight loss without the burden of extensive tracking.

The Science Behind Zero Point Foods

Zero-point foods are chosen based on their ability to keep you full and satisfied longer. They often have a high water and fiber content, which promotes fullness and helps control hunger levels. For instance, eating a large salad with lean protein and a variety of vegetables can fill you up without a high calorie count. Additionally, the body naturally burns more calories digesting protein compared to carbohydrates or fats, making protein-rich zero-point foods particularly effective.

Why Zero Point Foods Are Effective for Weight Loss

1. Simplicity and Flexibility: One of the biggest challenges in any diet is maintaining consistency. Zero-point foods make meal planning easier, as you don't need to worry about counting points or calories meticulously. This simplicity allows for greater adherence to the plan over time.
2. Balanced Nutrition: Zero-point foods ensure you're not just eating fewer calories but also getting the vitamins and minerals your body needs to function optimally. By choosing zero-point foods, you can create balanced, nutrient-rich meals that support both weight loss and overall health.
3. Encourages Whole, Unprocessed Eating: Most zero-point foods are whole and minimally processed. By building meals around these ingredients, you naturally reduce your intake of added sugars, unhealthy fats, and refined carbs, which can contribute to weight gain and other health issues.

4. Supports Long-Term Lifestyle Changes: Zero-point eating isn't a crash diet. It's a sustainable way of eating that you can maintain for the long term. This approach helps you build habits that prioritize nutritious food choices without feeling restrictive.

Benefits of a Zero Point Diet

The zero-point diet approach is celebrated for its simplicity, flexibility, and effectiveness in promoting weight management and overall well-being. By focusing on zero-point foods as the core of your meals, you can enjoy various benefits that make this diet both sustainable and rewarding. Here's an in-depth look at why adopting a zero-point diet can be transformative for your health journey.

1. Promotes Natural, Unrestricted Eating

One of the most appealing aspects of a zero-point diet is that it encourages natural and unrestricted eating patterns. Unlike traditional diets that often impose strict calorie counting or portion control, a zero-point diet allows you to eat freely from a wide range of wholesome foods. This promotes a healthier relationship with food, where you feel more focused on nourishment rather than limitations.

2. Supports Weight Loss and Maintenance

A zero-point diet can be highly effective for weight loss and weight maintenance due to the types of foods it includes. Zero-point foods are typically low in calories but high in fiber and water content, making them filling without significantly increasing your calorie intake. This means you can create meals that are satisfying and substantial, reducing the likelihood of overeating and supporting sustainable weight loss.

How This Helps:

- Increased Satiety: Foods like vegetables, fruits, and lean proteins help keep you fuller for longer, curbing hunger and reducing the need for frequent snacking.
- Reduced Caloric Density: The low-calorie nature of these foods allows for generous portion sizes without the added calories, making it easier to manage your intake naturally.

3. Encourages Healthy Habits

A zero-point diet inherently promotes the consumption of whole, unprocessed foods, which are key to long-term health and wellness. By building your meals around zero-point foods, you're more likely to adopt habits that benefit not only your weight but your overall health.

Benefits for Your Health:

- Nutrient-Dense Choices: Zero-point foods are packed with essential vitamins, minerals, and antioxidants that support immune function, energy levels, and general well-being.

- Balanced Nutrition: Because the diet emphasizes diverse food groups like lean proteins, fruits, vegetables, and legumes, you get a range of nutrients essential for bodily functions.

4. Reduces Food-Related Stress and Anxiety

Food-related stress, often driven by restrictive eating plans or fear of exceeding calorie limits, can be a significant barrier to maintaining a healthy diet. The zero-point system takes away the need for constant monitoring, providing a sense of freedom while still allowing for effective weight management.

Mental Health Benefits:

- Less Pressure: Knowing you can eat freely from an extensive list of zero-point foods helps remove the stress associated with meal planning.
- Improved Relationship with Food: When eating becomes less about strict numbers and more about nourishing your body, it fosters a positive attitude toward food and eating.

5. Adaptable to Various Lifestyles and Dietary Needs

Whether you're following a plant-based, pescatarian, or traditional diet, the zero-point plan is flexible enough to adapt to different lifestyles. It accommodates a variety of preferences and dietary restrictions, making it easier to stick to in the long run.

Customizable for All Diets:

- Vegetarian and Vegan Options: Many plant-based proteins, vegetables, and fruits are zero-point foods, making it simple to build meals that align with vegan or vegetarian diets.
- Low-Carb and High-Protein Choices: For those seeking higher protein intake or fewer carbs, lean proteins and non-starchy vegetables can be emphasized.
- Family-Friendly: You can integrate zero-point meals that the whole family will enjoy, making it easier to maintain your diet in a household setting.

6. Boosts Long-Term Success and Sustainability

Diets that are overly restrictive or hard to maintain often lead to short-term results followed by a return to old habits. The zero-point diet is different. It's designed to be a sustainable way of eating that you can maintain over the long term. By encouraging balance and moderation, it sets you up for lasting success.

Why It Works:

- Sustainable Practices: Focusing on foods that don't require portion control or calorie counting makes it easier to build habits you can stick to.
- Balanced Approach: While zero-point foods are the foundation, there's room to incorporate other food types in moderation, making the diet adaptable and more enjoyable.
- Encourages Lifelong Learning: The more you work with zero-point foods, the better you become at recognizing healthy choices and integrating them seamlessly into your routine.

7. Promotes Overall Wellness Beyond Weight Loss

Although weight management is often the primary goal, a zero-point diet does more than help you shed pounds. It contributes to better overall health by emphasizing whole, nutritious foods that support various bodily functions and reduce the risk of chronic diseases.

Key Health Perks:

- Heart Health: Lean proteins and vegetables can help manage cholesterol levels and support cardiovascular health.
- Digestive Benefits: High-fiber foods promote good digestion and help maintain a healthy gut.
- Steady Energy Levels: By focusing on nutrient-rich options, you'll experience fewer energy spikes and crashes throughout the day.

Common Myths and Misconceptions

The concept of zero-point eating is simple and effective, yet it is sometimes misunderstood due to misinformation and myths. To ensure you start your zero-point diet with accurate knowledge and realistic expectations, let's address some of the most common myths and misconceptions.

Myth 1: Zero Point Foods Mean Unlimited Eating Without Consequences

The Reality: While zero-point foods can be enjoyed more freely than high-calorie or processed options, they should still be consumed mindfully. These foods are chosen for their low-calorie density, high fiber content, and ability to promote fullness, but overindulging in any food can lead to an imbalance in your diet and, potentially, weight gain.

Clarification: Zero-point foods are a tool to help you manage hunger and build satisfying meals without constantly counting calories. However, listening to your body's hunger and fullness cues is important to ensure balanced eating.

Myth 2: All Zero Point Foods Are Low in Calories

The Reality: Not all zero-point foods are extremely low in calories. For instance, some legumes and fruits can contain a moderate amount of calories, but they are still classified as zero points due to their high fiber and nutrient content. The zero-point system is not solely about calorie counts but about encouraging choices that fill you up and nourish your body.

Clarification: Zero-point foods are chosen for their overall nutritional benefits and impact on satiety, not just their calorie content. Incorporating these foods into your diet supports balanced meals, but moderation and portion awareness are key for achieving long-term goals.

Myth 3: Zero Point Foods Are "Free" and Can Be Eaten Without Limit

The Reality: The idea that zero-point foods are completely "free" can be misleading. The term zero point simply means that these foods don't count toward your daily point allocation in some weight management programs. However, they still contain calories and should be part of a balanced diet.

Clarification: While you don't need to track zero-point foods as strictly, they should be

part of a varied diet that includes other nutrients, such as healthy fats and whole grains, to maintain balance and avoid nutritional gaps.

Myth 4: Zero Point Foods Are the Same for Everyone

The Reality: Not all weight management programs have the same zero-point foods, and individual dietary needs can vary. Factors such as dietary preferences, health conditions, and nutritional goals can influence what foods are considered zero points for different individuals.

Clarification: While there are common zero-point food categories like lean proteins, fruits, and vegetables, it's essential to customize your approach based on your own dietary requirements. For example, some people may need to limit certain fruits or legumes due to specific health conditions.

Myth 5: You Can't Lose Weight Eating Zero Point Foods

The Reality: One misconception is that because zero-point foods don't need to be tracked, they won't contribute to weight loss. In fact, zero-point foods are specifically chosen for their ability to aid in weight management due to their nutrient density and satiating properties.

Clarification: Many people have successfully used a zero-point approach as part of a balanced diet to lose weight and maintain their results. The key is to focus on zero-point foods as the base of your meals while incorporating other healthy food options in moderation.

Myth 6: Zero Point Foods Are Boring and Bland

The Reality: Another myth is that a zero-point diet is restrictive and flavorless. This couldn't be further from the truth. Zero-point foods include a wide variety of options, from juicy fruits and crisp vegetables to flavorful lean proteins and hearty legumes.

Clarification: With the right preparation techniques and seasonings, zero-point foods can be delicious and satisfying. Spices, herbs, citrus, and other natural flavor enhancers can transform simple ingredients into mouthwatering meals. This cookbook is packed with recipes that demonstrate just how versatile and exciting zero-point meals can be.

Myth 7: Zero Point Foods Lack Nutritional Value

The Reality: Some people think zero-point foods are chosen just for being low in calories and don't provide substantial nutrition. In reality, most zero-point foods are nutrient-dense and full of essential vitamins, minerals, and antioxidants that support overall health.

Clarification: Zero-point foods include powerhouses like leafy greens, berries, fish, and legumes, which are known for their health benefits. When combined with other nutrient-dense foods, they create balanced meals that help meet your body's nutritional needs.

Myth 8: You Can't Get Enough Protein on a Zero Point Diet

The Reality: Concerns about protein intake can be common when starting a zero-point diet, but there are plenty of zero-point options that provide sufficient protein. Lean meats, fish, eggs, and plant-based sources like tofu and lentils all offer high-quality protein without counting toward your daily points.

Clarification: By including these protein-rich zero-point foods in your meals, you can meet your protein needs without sacrificing taste or variety. Pairing these with non-zero-point foods like healthy fats and whole grains ensures a complete and balanced diet.

Myth 9: Zero Point Eating Is Only for Weight Loss

The Reality: While the zero-point diet is popular for weight management, its benefits extend beyond just losing weight. It encourages a focus on whole, unprocessed foods, making it a valuable approach for anyone looking to adopt healthier eating habits, manage blood sugar levels, or maintain an active lifestyle.

Clarification: The zero-point approach promotes eating patterns that support general wellness. By focusing on nutrient-rich, filling foods, you're helping your body thrive in various ways, from improved digestion and energy levels to better heart health.

Transitioning to a Zero Point Lifestyle

Transitioning to a zero-point lifestyle can feel exciting yet unfamiliar at first. With a few strategic steps and the right mindset, you can ease into this way of eating and create habits that will support your health goals over the long term. Here's a detailed guide to help you transition smoothly and make the most of your zero-point journey.

1. Start by Understanding Zero Point Foods

Before diving into meal planning, it's essential to familiarize yourself with the concept of zero-point foods. Understanding why certain foods are designated as zero points will give you confidence in your choices and help you build meals that align with your goals.

Tips for Learning:

- Review Food Lists: Study the categories of zero-point foods, such as lean proteins, non-starchy vegetables, fruits, and legumes.
- Know the Benefits: Keep in mind that zero-point foods are nutrient-dense, filling, and contribute to better overall health.

2. Assess Your Current Eating Habits

Evaluating your current eating habits will give you insight into where changes can be made to integrate zero-point foods. Take note of the meals and snacks you already enjoy and identify areas where zero-point foods can be incorporated.

Steps to Assess:

- Keep a Food Diary: Track your meals for a few days to see which foods align with zero points and where you might need adjustments.
- Identify Gaps: Determine if you're lacking in certain food groups, such as vegetables or lean proteins, and make a plan to include them more often.

3. Stock Your Kitchen with Essentials

Having a well-stocked kitchen is key to transitioning smoothly into a zero-point lifestyle. Fill your pantry, fridge, and freezer with essential zero-point foods so that you're always prepared to make a healthy choice.

Kitchen Staples to Have:

- Fresh Produce: Leafy greens, tomatoes, cucumbers, berries, and apples.
- Proteins: Skinless chicken breast, eggs, fish, tofu, and legumes like lentils and chickpeas.
- Flavor Enhancers: Herbs, spices, lemon juice, and vinegar for adding taste without extra points.

Pro Tip: Prep and wash produce in advance so that it's ready for snacking or cooking, saving you time during the week.

5. Embrace Flexibility and Adapt Recipes

Transitioning to a zero-point lifestyle doesn't mean giving up your favorite meals. Instead, adapt recipes to include more zero-point foods or find creative ways to lighten up dishes you already love.

Adapting Tips:

- Swap Ingredients: Replace high-point ingredients with zero-point alternatives, like swapping pasta for zucchini noodles or rice for cauliflower rice.
- Enhance with Flavor: Use spices, herbs, and citrus to add zest and depth to your meals without adding points.

6. Practice Mindful Eating

While zero-point foods don't need to be tracked as closely, mindful eating is still essential. Paying attention to how you feel while eating can help you tune into your hunger and fullness cues and avoid overeating.

Mindful Eating Strategies:

- Eat Slowly: Take your time to savor each bite, allowing your body to recognize when it's full.
- Avoid Distractions: Try to eat without the TV or your phone so you can focus on enjoying your meal.
- Check In with Yourself: Pause halfway through your meal to assess your hunger level and decide if you need to continue eating.

7. Set Realistic Goals and Celebrate Progress

Transitioning to a zero-point lifestyle is a process that takes time. Set achievable goals for yourself, such as trying a new zero-point recipe each week or meal prepping for a few days at a time. Celebrate small milestones to stay motivated and positive about your progress.

Goal-Setting Tips:

- Start with One Meal a Day: Begin by making breakfast or lunch entirely zero points, and gradually increase to more meals.

- Track Progress: Keep a journal or use an app to record your meals, note how you feel, and highlight any successes.

8. Be Patient and Kind to Yourself

As with any new way of eating, there may be an adjustment period. Be patient with yourself as you learn and make changes. It's natural to have days that don't go perfectly, but what matters most is your commitment to progress over time.

Reminders:

- Don't Stress Over Perfection: Focus on making better choices consistently rather than achieving perfection.
- Adjust as Needed: Your diet should fit your lifestyle, not the other way around. Make modifications to suit your needs and preferences.

Essential Ingredients and Pantry Staples

Budget-Friendly Essentials for Your Zero Point Pantry

Stocking your pantry with essential ingredients is key to making the zero-point lifestyle easy, accessible, and affordable. With a well-organized pantry, you can create satisfying meals quickly without needing to make frequent grocery runs. Here's a list of budget-friendly zero-point essentials to keep on hand for delicious and nutritious meal options.

1. Fresh Vegetables

- Leafy Greens: Spinach, kale, arugula, and lettuce are versatile for salads, smoothies, and cooking.
- Cruciferous Vegetables: Broccoli, cauliflower, and Brussels sprouts are filling, fiber-rich options that work well in various dishes.
- Root Vegetables: Carrots, radishes, and turnips add crunch and can be used in soups, stews, or roasted.
- Other Staples: Bell peppers, zucchini, cucumbers, and tomatoes are all zero-point vegetables that add flavor, texture, and nutrition to meals.

2. Fresh and Frozen Fruits

- Fresh Fruits: Apples, oranges, bananas, and berries are affordable and great for snacks, salads, and desserts.
- Frozen Fruits: Keep frozen berries, mangoes, and cherries on hand for smoothies, yogurt toppings, and easy desserts.

- Citrus Fruits: Lemons and limes are perfect for adding zest and acidity to dishes without extra points.

3. Lean Proteins

- Chicken Breast and Turkey: Skinless chicken and turkey breast are affordable, high-protein options that work in various recipes.
- Eggs: Eggs are a versatile, inexpensive protein that can be used in countless ways, from breakfast scrambles to salad toppings.
- Fish and Seafood: Cod, tilapia, shrimp, and canned tuna are all lean proteins that are budget-friendly and easy to cook.
- Tofu and Legumes: Tofu, black beans, chickpeas, and lentils are economical protein sources that can be used in stir-fries, soups, and salads.

4. Low-Fat Dairy and Dairy Alternatives

- Fat-Free Greek Yogurt: A creamy, protein-packed base for smoothies, dressings, and snacks.
- Unsweetened Almond Milk: A low-calorie, zero-point alternative to dairy milk.
- Cottage Cheese: Low-fat or fat-free cottage cheese provides protein and can be added to salads or served as a snack with fruit.

5. Herbs, Spices, and Flavor Enhancers

- Fresh and Dried Herbs: Basil, cilantro, parsley, thyme, and rosemary enhance flavor without adding points.
- Spices: Cinnamon, cumin, turmeric, garlic powder, and black pepper make your meals exciting and flavorful.
- Vinegars and Citrus: Balsamic vinegar, apple cider vinegar, and fresh citrus juice add acidity and zest, enhancing taste without extra points.

6. Low-Calorie Sauces and Condiments

- Salsa: Fresh or jarred salsa is a zero-point condiment perfect for salads, wraps, and dips.
- Mustard: Dijon or yellow mustard adds tang and spice to sandwiches, salads, and marinades.
- Hot Sauce and Soy Sauce: Both can be used sparingly to add heat and umami to dishes.

Ingredient Substitutions and Alternatives

One of the best ways to stick to a zero-point diet is to know how to swap out ingredients based on what you have available. This flexibility helps you save money and make meals with what's on hand.

Common Substitutions:

- Chicken Breast ↔ Turkey Breast: Both are lean proteins with similar flavors and can be used interchangeably.
- Zucchini Noodles ↔ Cauliflower Rice: These are great low-carb swaps for pasta or rice and can be customized with spices or sauces.
- Greek Yogurt ↔ Cottage Cheese: Both provide creaminess and protein, perfect for dips, dressings, or as a breakfast base.
- Leafy Greens ↔ Cabbage or Lettuce: If you're out of one green, cabbage or lettuce are great substitutes in salads and wraps.

Healthy Alternatives:

- Rice: Swap rice with cauliflower rice or quinoa for a zero-point or low-point option.
- Pasta: Try zucchini noodles or spaghetti squash instead of traditional pasta.
- Sour Cream: Use fat-free Greek yogurt in place of sour cream for a zero-point, creamy topping.

Pro Tip: Always keep frozen vegetables and fruits on hand. They're just as nutritious as fresh options and last longer, making them ideal for quick meal prep.

How to Shop Smart and Save Money

Eating healthy doesn't have to be expensive. With a few strategic shopping habits, you can stick to a zero-point diet on a budget.

1. Buy in Bulk

- Purchasing items like beans, grains, and spices in bulk can save money. Use bulk bins for dried beans, lentils, and other pantry staples that you can store long-term.
- Frozen Produce: Stock up on frozen fruits and vegetables, which are often cheaper than fresh and don't spoil quickly.

2. Shop Seasonally

- In-season produce is typically more affordable and flavorful. Plan your meals around fruits and vegetables that are in season to save money and add variety.
- Local Markets: Farmers' markets and local produce stands often have fresher and cheaper options compared to supermarkets.

3. Use Store Brands

- Opt for store-brand items, which are often less expensive than name brands but just as high in quality. Items like canned beans, frozen veggies, and dairy products are great places to look for savings.

4. Plan Your Meals and Make a List

- Write down the recipes you want to make for the week and list the ingredients you need. Sticking to a list helps prevent impulse buys and keeps you focused on essentials.
- Organize by Store Section: Group your list by produce, pantry items, and proteins so you can shop efficiently and avoid overspending.

5. Avoid Processed and Pre-Packaged Foods

- While convenient, pre-packaged foods are usually more expensive. By focusing on whole foods like fresh vegetables, fruits, and proteins, you'll stretch your budget and eat healthier.

6. Batch Cook and Freeze Leftovers

- Cooking in larger batches and freezing leftovers allows you to have zero-point meals ready without extra effort. Soups, stews, and casseroles are especially freezer-friendly and can be portioned out for future meals.

Pro Tip: Consider investing in a slow cooker or pressure cooker to make batch cooking easier and more efficient.

With these budget-friendly essentials, substitutions, and money-saving tips, your zero-point pantry will be ready for any meal. Stocking up on versatile ingredients means you'll always have the foundation for healthy, delicious meals at home.

Tips for Making the Most of This Cookbook

To fully benefit from *Super Easy Zero Point Weight Loss Cookbook*, it helps to know how to best navigate and utilize the recipes, meal plans, and tips provided. This section will equip you with practical strategies to enhance your cooking experience, save time, and maintain motivation throughout your weight loss journey.

1. Start with the Basics

Before diving into the recipes, take a moment to review the chapters that introduce zero-point foods and their benefits. Understanding the principles behind zero-point eating will give you a strong foundation and help you make informed choices as you plan your meals.

2. Plan Ahead with the 60-Day Meal Plan

One of the key features of this cookbook is the comprehensive 60-day meal plan. Planning your meals ahead of time is crucial for staying consistent, saving time, and avoiding impulse eating. Here's how to make the most of it:

- Customize Your Plan: While the meal plan is designed to be balanced, feel free to swap meals or adjust recipes to better suit your preferences and dietary needs.
- Batch Cooking and Meal Prep: Consider preparing certain elements of your meals in advance, such as chopping vegetables or marinating proteins, to make cooking during the week quicker and easier.
- Create Weekly Shopping Lists: The meal plan includes weekly shopping lists to help streamline your grocery trips. Check your pantry before shopping to avoid buying items you already have.

3. Master the Art of Ingredient Substitution

This cookbook is filled with flexible recipes that allow for ingredient swaps to suit your tastes, dietary restrictions, or available pantry items. Here are some quick tips:

- Substitute Proteins: Swap chicken for turkey, tofu, or fish depending on what you have on hand or prefer.
- Adjust Flavor Profiles: Feel free to tweak spices or herbs to match your palate.
- Budget-Friendly Alternatives: If certain ingredients are costly or unavailable, use similar items that are more accessible (e.g., substitute spinach for kale or use canned beans instead of fresh).

4. Incorporate Nutritional Information

Each recipe in this cookbook comes with detailed nutritional information, including serving sizes and macro breakdowns. This can be particularly helpful for those looking to manage specific dietary goals, such as protein intake or calorie awareness. Use this information to:

- Track Your Nutritional Goals: If you're following a specific nutritional plan, these details will help you stay on track.
- Adjust Portions Accordingly: Knowing the nutritional content allows you to adjust portion sizes to fit your dietary needs.

5. Use Recipes as a Framework

While each recipe provides step-by-step instructions, they're designed to be adaptable. Don't be afraid to make substitutions or add your twist to the recipes. For example:

- Add Vegetables for Extra Volume: Boost the nutritional value by adding extra zero-point vegetables to meals.
- Incorporate Your Favorite Flavors: Enhance the taste with your favorite herbs or a splash of citrus for a fresh twist.
- Make It Family-Friendly: Adapt the recipes to serve more people and incorporate side dishes that complement the main meal.

6. Balance Your Meals

Zero-point recipes are designed to keep you full and satisfied, but balance is essential for comprehensive nutrition. Here's how to build balanced meals:

- Include Healthy Fats: While many recipes focus on zero-point ingredients, consider adding healthy fats like avocado, olive oil, or nuts in moderation for a complete meal.
- Pair with Whole Grains: Include whole grains such as quinoa or brown rice to add fiber and keep you energized.
- Stay Hydrated: Pair meals with water, herbal teas, or other calorie-free beverages to stay hydrated and support digestion.

7. Stay Consistent and Keep It Simple

Consistency is key when adopting new eating habits. By sticking to the recipes and the meal plan provided, you'll develop routines that make healthy eating second nature. Here are a few final tips:

- Start Small: Begin with recipes that require fewer ingredients and shorter prep times if you're new to cooking.
- Mix It Up: Try different recipes each week to keep meals exciting and prevent diet fatigue.
- Celebrate Small Wins: Acknowledge your progress and the effort you put into making healthier choices. Whether it's trying a new recipe or sticking to your meal plan for the week, every step counts.

8. Engage the Whole Family

Involving your family in your weight loss journey can make the process more enjoyable and sustainable. Many recipes in this cookbook are designed to be family-friendly, so everyone can benefit from nutritious, zero-point meals. Share cooking duties or let your kids choose recipes to keep them engaged and excited about healthy eating.

9. Use the Troubleshooting Section

If you encounter challenges along the way, refer to the troubleshooting chapter at the end of the cookbook. It covers common questions, substitutions, and how to adapt recipes for various dietary needs.

Chapter 1

Breakfasts to Fuel Your Day

Savory Zero Point Omelet with Vegetables

 10 mins   5 mins   1

Ingredients:

- 2 large eggs or 1 egg + 2 egg whites
- ½ cup diced bell peppers (any color)
- ¼ cup chopped spinach
- ¼ cup diced tomatoes
- ¼ cup sliced mushrooms
- Salt and black pepper to taste
- Cooking spray

Procedure:

1. Heat a non-stick pan over medium heat and spray lightly with cooking spray.
2. Add the bell peppers, spinach, tomatoes, and mushrooms. Sauté for 2-3 minutes until vegetables are tender.
3. Whisk the eggs in a bowl and season with salt and pepper.
4. Pour the eggs over the sautéed vegetables and cook until the edges begin to set.
5. Fold the omelet in half and cook for another minute. Serve hot

Nutritional Info: Approx. 150 calories, 12g protein, 8g fat, 6g carbs.

Overnight Chia Seed Pudding

5 mins · 0 mins · 2

Ingredients:

- 2 tbsp chia seeds
- 1 cup unsweetened almond milk
- 1 tsp vanilla extract
- Fresh fruit for topping (optional)

Procedure:

1. Combine chia seeds, almond milk, and vanilla extract in a bowl or jar.
2. Stir well, cover, and refrigerate overnight.
3. In the morning, stir the pudding and top with fresh fruit before serving.

Nutritional Info: Approx. 90 calories, 3g protein, 4g fat, 10g carbs

Fresh Fruit Salad with a Twist

10 mins · 0 mins · 2

Ingredients:

- 1 cup strawberries, sliced
- ½ cup blueberries
- 1 kiwi, peeled and chopped
- 1 apple, cored and diced
- 2 tbsp fresh mint leaves, chopped
- Juice of 1 lime

Procedure:

1. Combine all the fruits in a bowl.
2. Add the chopped mint leaves and lime juice. Toss gently.
3. Serve chilled for a refreshing breakfast

Nutritional Info: Approx. 100 calories, 2g protein, 0.5g fat, 25g carbs.

Zucchini Pancakes with Herbs

 10 minutes   10 mins  4 small pancakes

Ingredients:

- 1 medium zucchini, grated and excess moisture removed
- 2 eggs, lightly beaten
- ¼ cup chopped green onions
- 2 tbsp fresh dill, chopped
- Salt and black pepper to taste
- Cooking spray

Procedure:

1. Combine grated zucchini, eggs, green onions, and dill in a bowl. Season with salt and black pepper.
2. Heat a non-stick skillet over medium heat and spray with cooking spray.
3. Spoon small portions of the batter onto the skillet and flatten slightly.
4. Cook for 3-4 minutes on each side until golden brown. Serve warm.

Nutritional Info: Approx. 80 calories per pancake, 5g protein, 3g fat, 7g carbs.

Spinach and Tomato Scramble

 5 mins   5 mins 1

Ingredients:

- 3 egg whites or 1 whole egg + 1 egg white
- ½ cup fresh spinach, chopped
- ¼ cup diced tomatoes
- Salt and black pepper to taste
- Cooking spray

Procedure:

1. Spray a non-stick skillet with cooking spray and heat over medium heat.
2. Add spinach and tomatoes; sauté for 1-2 minutes.
3. Pour in the eggs and scramble until cooked through. Season with salt and black pepper. Serve hot.

Nutritional Info: Approx. 70 calories, 10g protein, 2g fat, 4g carbs.

Oatmeal with Apple and Cinnamon

5 mins   5 mins   1

Ingredients:

- ½ cup quick oats
- 1 small apple, diced
- ½ tsp cinnamon
- 1 cup water or unsweetened almond milk

Procedure:

1. Combine oats, apple, and cinnamon in a saucepan with water or almond milk.
2. Cook over medium heat for 5 minutes, stirring occasionally until oats are tender.
3. Serve warm with an optional sprinkle of cinnamon on top.

Nutritional Info: Approx. 150 calories, 4g protein, 2g fat, 32g carbs.

Poached Eggs with Salsa

3 mins   3 mins   1

Ingredients:

- 2 eggs
- ½ cup salsa (homemade or store-bought)
- Fresh cilantro for garnish

Procedure:

1. Bring a pot of water to a simmer and gently crack the eggs into the water.
2. Cook for 3 minutes or until desired doneness.
3. Serve eggs over a bed of salsa and garnish with fresh cilantro.

Nutritional Info: Approx. 130 calories, 12g protein, 9g fat, 5g carbs.

Berry Smoothie Bowl

5 mins   0 mins   1

Ingredients:

- 1 cup frozen mixed berries
- ½ cup unsweetened almond milk
- 1 tbsp chia seeds
- Fresh berries and coconut flakes for topping (optional)

Procedure:

1. Blend the frozen berries, almond milk, and chia seeds until smooth.
2. Pour into a bowl and top with fresh berries and coconut flakes if desired.

Nutritional Info: Approx. 120 calories, 3g protein, 2g fat, 25g carbs.

Zero Point Banana Pancakes

5 mins   5 mins   3 small pancakes

Ingredients:

- 1 ripe banana, mashed
- 2 eggs
- ¼ tsp baking powder
- ½ tsp vanilla extract

Procedure:

1. Mix the mashed banana, eggs, baking powder, and vanilla extract in a bowl.
2. Heat a non-stick pan over medium heat and spoon the batter to make small pancakes.
3. Cook for 2-3 minutes per side until golden brown. Serve warm.

Nutritional Info: Approx. 150 calories, 8g protein, 4g fat, 25g carbs.

Breakfast Quinoa Bowl

5 mins   15 mins   1

Ingredients:

- ½ cup cooked quinoa
- 1 cup mixed berries
- 1 tbsp chia seeds
- 1 tsp honey (optional)

Procedure:

1. Combine the cooked quinoa, berries, and chia seeds in a bowl.
2. Drizzle with honey if desired and serve.

Nutritional Info: Approx. 200 calories, 6g protein, 3g fat, 38g carbs.

Spiced Pear Compote

5 mins   10 mins   2

Ingredients:

- 2 pears, peeled and diced
- ½ tsp cinnamon
- ¼ tsp nutmeg
- 2 tbsp water

Procedure:

1. Add the pears, cinnamon, nutmeg, and water to a saucepan.
2. Cook over medium heat for 10 minutes, stirring occasionally until pears are tender.
3. Serve warm or chilled as a topping for oatmeal or yogurt.

Nutritional Info: Approx. 80 calories, 1g protein, 0g fat, 20g carbs per serving..

Veggie Breakfast Burrito

10 *mins*   5 *mins*   1

Ingredients:

- 1 low-carb tortilla (optional)
- ½ cup egg whites
- ¼ cup diced bell peppers
- ¼ cup black beans
- 2 tbsp salsa

Procedure:

1. Cook the egg whites and bell peppers in a non-stick pan over medium heat.
2. Add the black beans and cook for an additional minute.
3. Spoon the mixture onto the tortilla, top with salsa, and wrap.

Nutritional Info: Approx. 120 calories, 10g protein, 2g fat, 20g carbs.

Lemon Ricotta Toast

5 *mins*   0 *mins*   1

Ingredients:

- 1 slice whole grain bread (optional)
- ¼ cup fat-free ricotta cheese
- Zest of 1 lemon
- Honey for drizzling (optional)

Procedure:

1. Toast the bread and spread the ricotta cheese evenly.
2. Sprinkle lemon zest on top and drizzle with honey if desired.

Nutritional Info: Approx. 100 calories, 7g protein, 1g fat, 15g carbs.

Grilled Pineapple Slices

5 mins   5 mins   2

Ingredients:

- ½ pineapple, peeled and sliced
- 1 tbsp lime juice

Procedure:

1. Heat a grill or grill pan over medium heat.
2. Place the pineapple slices on the grill and cook for 2-3 minutes on each side.
3. Drizzle with lime juice before serving

Nutritional Info: Approx. 60 calories, 1g protein, 0g fat, 15g carbs per serving.

Avocado and Egg Breakfast Bowl

5 mins   5 mins   1

Ingredients:

- 1 hard-boiled egg, sliced
- ½ avocado, diced
- ½ cup cherry tomatoes, halved
- ¼ cup diced cucumber
- Fresh herbs like basil or parsley for garnish
- Salt and black pepper to taste

Procedure:

1. Arrange the egg, avocado, tomatoes, and cucumber in a bowl.
2. Season with salt and black pepper and garnish with fresh herbs.
3. Enjoy as a refreshing, protein-packed start to your day.

Nutritional Info: Approx. 140 calories, 7g protein, 10g fat, 7g carbs.

Sweet Potato Breakfast Hash

5 mins   10 mins   2

Ingredients:

- 1 medium sweet potato, peeled and diced
- ½ bell pepper, diced
- ½ small onion, diced
- ½ cup black beans (optional)
- Salt, pepper, and paprika to taste
- Cooking spray

Procedure:

1. Heat a skillet over medium heat and coat with cooking spray.
2. Add the sweet potato and cook for 5 minutes, stirring occasionally.
3. Add the bell pepper, onion, and seasonings. Cook until the sweet potato is tender.
4. Stir in black beans if desired, and cook until heated through.

Nutritional Info: Approx. 120 calories, 3g protein, 1g fat, 26g carbs per serving.

Apple Cinnamon Yogurt Parfait

5 mins   0 mins   1

Ingredients:

- 1 cup fat-free Greek yogurt
- 1 small apple, diced
- ½ tsp cinnamon
- 1 tsp chia seeds (optional)

Procedure:

1. Layer the Greek yogurt and diced apple in a bowl or jar.
2. Sprinkle with cinnamon and chia seeds for added fiber and texture.
3. Serve chilled or at room temperature.

Nutritional Info: Approx. 90 calories, 10g protein, 0g fat, 15g carbs.

Mushroom and Spinach Breakfast Wrap

5 mins   5 mins   1

Ingredients:

- ½ cup egg whites or 1 whole egg + 1 egg white
- ¼ cup sliced mushrooms
- ¼ cup fresh spinach, chopped
- 1 whole grain wrap (optional)
- Salt and pepper to taste
- Cooking spray

Procedure:

1. Heat a non-stick pan over medium heat and spray with cooking spray.
2. Add the mushrooms and cook until softened, about 2 minutes.
3. Stir in the spinach and cook for another minute.
4. Add the egg whites, season with salt and pepper, and scramble until cooked through.
5. Spoon the mixture onto a wrap and roll up. Serve warm.

Nutritional Info: Approx. 100 calories, 12g protein, 2g fat, 10g carbs.

Tomato Basil Frittata

5 mins   10 mins   2

Ingredients:

- 3 large eggs
- ½ cup cherry tomatoes, halved
- ¼ cup fresh basil, chopped
- Salt and black pepper to taste
- Cooking spray

Procedure:

1. Preheat the oven to 350°F (180°C).
2. Whisk the eggs in a bowl, then stir in cherry tomatoes, basil, salt, and black pepper.
3. Coat an oven-safe skillet with cooking spray and pour the egg mixture in.
4. Cook on the stovetop over medium heat for 2-3 minutes, then transfer to the oven.
5. Bake for 5-7 minutes or until the eggs are set. Slice and serve.

Nutritional Info: Approx. 120 calories, 10g protein, 6g fat, 4g carbs per serving.

Chapter 2

Satisfying Lunches

Hearty Vegetable Soup with Herbs

10 mins   25   4

Ingredients:

- 1 large onion, chopped
- 2 carrots, diced
- 2 celery stalks, diced
- 2 cups chopped cabbage
- 1 zucchini, chopped
- 3 cups vegetable broth (low sodium)
- 1 tsp dried thyme
- 1 tsp dried oregano
- Salt and black pepper to taste

Procedure:

1. In a large pot, sauté the onion, carrots, and celery over medium heat for 5 minutes.

2. Add the cabbage, zucchini, vegetable broth, thyme, and oregano.

3. Bring to a boil, then reduce heat and simmer for 20 minutes.

4. Season with salt and black pepper before serving.

Nutritional Info: Approx. 80 calories per serving, 2g protein, 1g fat, 16g carbs.

Grilled Chicken and Spinach Salad

10 *mins*   15 *mins*   2

Ingredients:

- 2 boneless, skinless chicken breasts
- 4 cups fresh spinach
- 1 cup cherry tomatoes, halved
- 1 cucumber, sliced
- ½ red onion, thinly sliced
- Lemon wedges for garnish
- Salt and black pepper to taste
- Cooking spray

Procedure:

1. Season the chicken breasts with salt and black pepper.
2. Grill the chicken over medium heat for 7-8 minutes on each side or until fully cooked.
3. Let the chicken rest for 5 minutes before slicing.
4. Arrange spinach, tomatoes, cucumber, and red onion on plates. Top with sliced chicken and serve with lemon wedges.

Nutritional Info: Approx. 200 calories per serving, 30g protein, 4g fat, 12g carbs.

Zesty Mint Chutney Wraps

10 *mins*   0 *mins*   2

Ingredients:

- 4 large lettuce leaves (for wraps)
- 1 cup shredded chicken breast (pre-cooked)
- 2 tbsp mint chutney
- 1 small cucumber, julienned
- 1 small carrot, julienned

Procedure:

1. Mix the shredded chicken with mint chutney in a bowl.
2. Lay out the lettuce leaves and distribute the chicken mixture evenly.
3. Top with cucumber and carrot juliennes.
4. Roll up the lettuce leaves and serve.

Nutritional Info: Approx. 150 calories per serving, 22g protein, 2g fat, 10g carbs.

Mediterranean Chickpea Salad

10 mins   0 mins   4

Ingredients:

- 1 can (15 oz) chickpeas, drained and rinsed
- 1 cup cherry tomatoes, halved
- 1 cucumber, diced
- ¼ cup red onion, finely chopped
- ¼ cup fresh parsley, chopped
- Juice of 1 lemon
- Salt and black pepper to taste

Procedure:

1. In a large bowl, combine chickpeas, cherry tomatoes, cucumber, red onion, and parsley.
2. Drizzle lemon juice over the mixture and season with salt and black pepper.
3. Toss to combine and serve chilled.

Nutritional Info: Approx. 140 calories per serving, 5g protein, 2g fat, 25g carbs.

Zero Point Lentil Curry

10 mins   25   4

Ingredients:

- 1 cup red lentils
- 1 large onion, chopped
- 2 tomatoes, diced
- 2 cups vegetable broth
- 1 tsp curry powder
- ½ tsp cumin
- Salt to taste

Procedure:

1. Rinse the lentils and set aside.
2. In a pot, sauté the onion for 3-4 minutes until translucent.
3. Add tomatoes, curry powder, and cumin. Cook for 2 more minutes.
4. Add the lentils and vegetable broth, and bring to a boil.
5. Reduce heat and simmer for 20 minutes. Season with salt and serve.

Nutritional Info: Approx. 180 calories per serving, 12g protein, 0.5g fat, 30g carbs.

Cucumber and Tomato Salad with Basil

5 mins · 0 mins · 2

Ingredients:

- 2 cucumbers, sliced
- 2 tomatoes, diced
- ¼ cup fresh basil leaves, torn
- 1 tbsp balsamic vinegar
- Salt and black pepper to taste

Procedure:

1. Combine cucumbers, tomatoes, and basil in a bowl.
2. Drizzle with balsamic vinegar and season with salt and black pepper.
3. Toss gently and serve.

Nutritional Info: Approx. 60 calories per serving, 2g protein, 0.5g fat, 14g carbs.

Chicken Lettuce Wraps

10 mins · `10 mins · 4

Ingredients:

- 2 cups cooked, shredded chicken breast
- 1 tbsp low-sodium soy sauce
- 1 tsp ginger, grated
- 2 green onions, chopped
- 8 large lettuce leaves

Procedure:

1. In a bowl, mix the chicken, soy sauce, ginger, and green onions.
2. Spoon the chicken mixture into the lettuce leaves and serve.

Nutritional Info: Approx. 120 calories per serving, 20g protein, 2g fat, 6g carbs.

Cauliflower Fried Rice

10 mins   10 mins   2

Ingredients:

- 2 cups riced cauliflower
- 1 egg, beaten
- 1 cup mixed vegetables (carrots, peas, corn)
- 2 tbsp low-sodium soy sauce
- Green onions for garnish

Procedure:

1. Heat a non-stick pan and scramble the egg. Set aside.
2. Add the riced cauliflower and mixed vegetables to the pan and sauté for 5 minutes.
3. Stir in the scrambled egg and soy sauce. Cook for 2 more minutes.
4. Serve hot with green onions as garnish

Nutritional Info: Approx. 100 calories per serving, 5g protein, 3g fat, 15g carbs.

Broccoli and Lemon Zest Stir-Fry

5 mins   10 mins   2

Ingredients:

- 2 cups broccoli florets
- 1 clove garlic, minced
- Zest of 1 lemon
- 1 tbsp lemon juice
- Salt and black pepper to taste
- Cooking spray

Procedure:

1. Heat a pan over medium heat and spray with cooking spray.
2. Add garlic and sauté for 1 minute.
3. Add broccoli and stir-fry for 5-6 minutes.
4. Sprinkle lemon zest and lemon juice, and season with salt and pepper. Serve hot.

Nutritional Info: Approx. 70 calories per serving, 4g protein, 1g fat, 14g carbs.

Stuffed Bell Peppers with Quinoa

10 *mins*   25 *mins*   4

Ingredients:

- 2 large bell peppers, halved and seeded
- 1 cup cooked quinoa
- 1 cup black beans, drained and rinsed
- ½ cup diced tomatoes
- 1 tsp cumin
- Salt and black pepper to taste

Procedure:

1. Preheat oven to 375°F (190°C).
2. In a bowl, mix quinoa, black beans, tomatoes, cumin, salt, and black pepper.
3. Stuff the bell peppers with the quinoa mixture and place them in a baking dish.
4. Bake for 20-25 minutes or until peppers are tender. Serve warm.

Nutritional Info: Approx. 180 calories per serving, 8g protein, 2g fat, 35g carbs.

Asian Sesame Slaw

10 *mins*   0 *mins*   4

Ingredients:

- 2 cups shredded cabbage
- 1 cup shredded carrots
- 1 red bell pepper, thinly sliced
- 2 tbsp rice vinegar
- 1 tbsp low-sodium soy sauce
- 1 tbsp sesame seeds
- 1 tsp grated ginger

Procedure:

1. In a large bowl, combine cabbage, carrots, and bell pepper.
2. In a small bowl, mix rice vinegar, soy sauce, and grated ginger.
3. Pour the dressing over the vegetables and toss to coat.
4. Sprinkle sesame seeds on top and serve chilled.

Nutritional Info: Approx. 60 calories per serving, 2g protein, 2g fat, 12g carbs.

Roasted Beet Salad with Arugula

10 mins   25 mins   2

Ingredients:

- 2 medium beets, peeled and diced
- 2 cups arugula
- ¼ cup crumbled feta cheese (optional)
- 1 tbsp balsamic vinegar
- Salt and black pepper to taste

Procedure:

1. Preheat oven to 400°F (200°C). Place diced beets on a baking sheet and roast for 25 minutes or until tender.
2. Let the beets cool and mix with arugula in a bowl.
3. Drizzle balsamic vinegar over the salad and toss to coat.
4. Top with crumbled feta cheese if desired.

Nutritional Info: Approx. 90 calories per serving, 3g protein, 1.5g fat, 18g carbs.

Tuna and White Bean Salad

10 mins   0 mins   2

Ingredients:

- 1 can (5 oz) tuna in water, drained
- 1 can (15 oz) white beans, drained and rinsed
- 1 cup cherry tomatoes, halved
- 2 tbsp fresh parsley, chopped
- Juice of 1 lemon
- Salt and black pepper to taste

Procedure:

1. In a large bowl, combine tuna, white beans, cherry tomatoes, and parsley.
2. Drizzle lemon juice over the mixture and season with salt and black pepper.
3. Toss gently and serve.

Nutritional Info: Approx. 180 calories per serving, 25g protein, 1g fat, 25g carbs.

Zero Point Minestrone Soup

15 mins   30 mins   4

Ingredients:

- 1 large onion, chopped
- 2 carrots, diced
- 2 celery stalks, diced
- 1 zucchini, diced
- 1 cup green beans, chopped
- 1 can (14 oz) diced tomatoes
- 4 cups vegetable broth
- 1 tsp Italian seasoning
- 1 cup cooked chickpeas

Procedure:

1. In a large pot, sauté the onion, carrots, and celery for 5 minutes.
2. Add zucchini, green beans, diced tomatoes, vegetable broth, and Italian seasoning.
3. Simmer for 25 minutes. Add chickpeas in the last 5 minutes.
4. Serve hot.

Nutritional Info: Approx. 140 calories per serving, 5g protein, 1g fat, 28g carbs.

Sweet Potato and Black Bean Bowl

10 mins   20 mins   2

Ingredients:

- 1 large sweet potato, peeled and cubed
- 1 can (15 oz) black beans, drained and rinsed
- 1 avocado, sliced (optional)
- 1 tbsp lime juice
- 1 tsp cumin
- Salt and black pepper to taste

Procedure:

1. Boil or roast sweet potato cubes until tender.
2. In a bowl, combine sweet potatoes and black beans.
3. Add cumin, lime juice, salt, and black pepper. Toss gently.
4. Top with avocado slices if desired and serve.

Nutritional Info: Approx. 220 calories per serving, 8g protein, 3g fat, 45g carbs.

Tomato Basil Gazpacho

 15 mins   0 mins   4

Ingredients:

- 4 large tomatoes, chopped
- 1 cucumber, peeled and chopped
- 1 bell pepper, chopped
- 2 garlic cloves, minced
- ¼ cup fresh basil leaves
- 2 tbsp red wine vinegar
- Salt and black pepper to taste

Procedure:

1. In a blender, combine tomatoes, cucumber, bell pepper, garlic, and basil.
2. Add red wine vinegar and blend until smooth.
3. Season with salt and black pepper. Serve chilled.

Nutritional Info: Approx. 100 calories per serving, 3g protein, 1g fat, 20g carbs.

Shrimp and Avocado Salad

 10 mins   5 mins   2

Ingredients:

- 1 cup cooked shrimp
- 1 avocado, diced
- 1 cup mixed greens
- 1 tbsp lemon juice
- Salt and black pepper to taste

Procedure:

1. Combine shrimp, avocado, and mixed greens in a bowl.
2. Drizzle lemon juice over the salad and toss gently.
3. Season with salt and black pepper before serving.

Nutritional Info: Approx. 200 calories per serving, 15g protein, 12g fat, 10g carbs

Spaghetti Squash Primavera

10 *mins*   30 *mins*   4

Ingredients:

- 1 spaghetti squash, halved and seeds removed
- 1 zucchini, diced
- 1 bell pepper, diced
- 1 cup cherry tomatoes, halved
- 2 cloves garlic, minced
- Salt and black pepper to taste

Procedure:

1. Preheat oven to 400°F (200°C). Roast spaghetti squash for 30 minutes, cut-side down.
2. Scrape the cooked squash into strands with a fork.
3. In a pan, sauté garlic, zucchini, bell pepper, and cherry tomatoes for 5 minutes.
   Mix the squash strands with the sautéed vegetables and season with salt and black

Nutritional Info: Approx. 110 calories per serving, 3g protein, 1g fat, 24g carbs.

Lemon-Garlic Chicken Skewers

10 *mins*   15 *mins*   4

Ingredients:

- 2 chicken breasts, cut into cubes
- 2 tbsp lemon juice
- 2 cloves garlic, minced
- Salt and black pepper to taste
- Skewers

Procedure:

1. Marinate chicken cubes in lemon juice, garlic, salt, and black pepper for 10 minutes.
2. Thread the chicken onto skewers.
3. Grill over medium heat for 12-15 minutes, turning occasionally, until cooked through.
4. Serve hot with a side of vegetables or salad.

Nutritional Info: Approx. 180 calories per serving, 30g protein, 2g fat, 2g carbs.

Chapter 3
Wholesome Dinners

Baked Lemon Herb Fish with Steamed Vegetables

 10 mins   15 mins   2

Ingredients:

- 2 white fish fillets (e.g., cod or tilapia)
- 2 tbsp lemon juice
- 1 tsp dried thyme
- 1 tsp dried rosemary
- Salt and black pepper to taste
- Steamed mixed vegetables for serving

Procedure:

1. Preheat the oven to 400°F (200°C).
2. Season the fish fillets with lemon juice, thyme, rosemary, salt, and black pepper.
3. Place fish on a lined baking sheet and bake for 12-15 minutes or until the fish flakes easily with a fork.
4. Serve with steamed vegetables.

Nutritional Info: Approx. 150 calories per serving, 25g protein, 2g fat, 4g carbs.

Salsa Verde Chicken Bowls

10 mins   20 mins   2

Ingredients:

- 2 boneless, skinless chicken breasts
- ½ cup salsa verde
- 1 cup cooked brown rice (optional)
- Fresh cilantro for garnish

Procedure:

1. Preheat the oven to 375°F (190°C).
2. Place chicken breasts in a baking dish and pour salsa verde over them.
3. Bake for 20 minutes or until chicken is cooked through.
4. Serve over brown rice and garnish with cilantro.

Nutritional Info: Approx. 200 calories per serving, 30g protein, 2g fat, 10g carbs (without rice).

Zero Point Ratatouille

15 mins   30 mins   4

Ingredients:

- 1 eggplant, diced
- 1 zucchini, sliced
- 1 red bell pepper, chopped
- 1 onion, chopped
- 2 tomatoes, diced
- 1 tsp dried basil
- 1 tsp dried oregano
- Salt and black pepper to taste

Procedure:

1. Preheat oven to 400°F (200°C).
2. In a baking dish, combine all vegetables and season with basil, oregano, salt, and black pepper.
3. Bake for 30 minutes, stirring halfway through.
4. Serve warm.

Nutritional Info: Approx. 100 calories per serving, 3g protein, 1g fat, 20g carbs.

Turkey Meatballs with Marinara Sauce

10 mins   20 mins   4

Ingredients:

- 1 lb ground turkey
- 1 egg
- ½ cup chopped parsley
- 1 tsp garlic powder
- 1 cup marinara sauce (low sodium)
- Salt and black pepper to taste

Procedure:

1. Preheat oven to 400°F (200°C).
2. Mix ground turkey, egg, parsley, garlic powder, salt, and black pepper in a bowl.
3. Form into meatballs and place on a baking sheet.
4. Bake for 15 minutes. Pour marinara sauce over meatballs and bake for an additional 5 minutes.
5. Serve hot.

Nutritional Info: Approx. 180 calories per serving, 25g protein, 6g fat, 10g carbs.

Spinach-Stuffed Portobello Mushrooms

10 mins   15 mins   2

Ingredients:

- 4 large Portobello mushroom caps
- 1 cup cooked spinach, drained
- ¼ cup low-fat ricotta cheese
- 1 garlic clove, minced
- Salt and black pepper to taste

Procedure:

1. Preheat oven to 375°F (190°C).
2. Mix spinach, ricotta cheese, and minced garlic in a bowl. Season with salt and black pepper.
3. Fill each mushroom cap with the spinach mixture and place on a baking sheet.
4. Bake for 15 minutes and serve warm.

Nutritional Info: Approx. 120 calories per serving, 10g protein, 3g fat, 14g carbs.

Herb-Roasted Chicken Thighs

5 mins   30   4

Ingredients:

- 4 chicken thighs (skinless)
- 1 tsp dried rosemary
- 1 tsp dried thyme
- 2 cloves garlic, minced
- Salt and black pepper to taste

Procedure:

1. Preheat oven to 400°F (200°C).
2. Season chicken thighs with rosemary, thyme, garlic, salt, and black pepper.
3. Place in a baking dish and roast for 30 minutes or until golden and cooked through.
   Serve with a side salad or steamed vegetables.

Nutritional Info: Approx. 200 calories per serving, 25g protein, 8g fat, 1g carbs

Grilled Zucchini Lasagna

15 mins   20 mins   4

Ingredients:

- 2 large zucchinis, sliced lengthwise
- 1 cup low-fat ricotta cheese
- 1 cup marinara sauce
- ½ cup shredded mozzarella cheese (optional)
- Salt and black pepper to taste

Procedure:

1. Preheat grill or grill pan over medium heat.
2. Grill zucchini slices for 2-3 minutes per side until tender.
3. In a baking dish, layer zucchini slices, ricotta cheese, and marinara sauce. Repeat layers and top with mozzarella cheese if desired.
4. Bake at 375°F (190°C) for 15 minutes. Serve hot.

Nutritional Info: Approx. 160 calories per serving, 10g protein, 5g fat, 20g carbs.

Balsamic-Glazed Chicken Breast

5 mins   15 mins   2

Ingredients:

- 2 chicken breasts
- 2 tbsp balsamic vinegar
- 1 tbsp honey (optional)
- Salt and black pepper to taste

Procedure:

1. Preheat oven to 375°F (190°C).
2. Season chicken breasts with salt and black pepper.
3. Place in a baking dish and brush with balsamic vinegar and honey.
4. Bake for 15 minutes or until cooked through.
5. Serve with roasted vegetables or a side salad.

Nutritional Info: Approx. 180 calories per serving, 28g protein, 2g fat, 8g carbs.

Lentil Shepherd's Pie

10 mins   30 mins   4

Ingredients:

- 1 cup cooked lentils
- 1 onion, chopped
- 2 carrots, diced
- 1 cup vegetable broth
- 2 cups mashed potatoes (optional)
- 1 tsp thyme
- Salt and black pepper to taste

Procedure:

1. Preheat oven to 375°F (190°C).
2. Sauté onion and carrots in a skillet for 5 minutes. Add lentils, vegetable broth, and thyme.
3. Pour the mixture into a baking dish and spread mashed potatoes on top.
4. Bake for 20 minutes. Serve hot

Nutritional Info: Approx. 250 calories per serving, 10g protein, 5g fat, 45g carbs.

Roasted Cauliflower Tacos

10 *mins*   20   4

Ingredients:

- 1 head of cauliflower, cut into florets
- 1 tsp smoked paprika
- ½ tsp cumin
- Corn tortillas (optional)
- Lime wedges for serving

Procedure:

1. Preheat oven to 400°F (200°C).
2. Toss cauliflower florets with smoked paprika and cumin. Spread on a baking sheet and roast for 20 minutes.
3. Assemble tacos with roasted cauliflower and serve with lime wedges.

Nutritional Info: Approx. 150 calories per serving, 5g protein, 4g fat, 25g carbs (without tortillas).

Eggplant Parmesan with Tomato Sauce

10 *mins*   25 *mins*   4

Ingredients:

- 1 large eggplant, sliced
- 1 cup marinara sauce
- ¼ cup grated Parmesan cheese
- 1 cup shredded mozzarella cheese (optional)

Procedure:

1. Preheat oven to 375°F (190°C).
2. Layer eggplant slices in a baking dish, covering with marinara sauce and sprinkling with Parmesan cheese.
3. Top with mozzarella if desired.
4. Bake for 25 minutes or until eggplant is tender. Serve warm.

Nutritional Info: Approx. 170 calories per serving, 7g protein, 5g fat, 20g carbs.

Cabbage Roll Casserole

15 mins   30 mins   4

Ingredients:

- 1 small head of cabbage, chopped
- 1 lb ground turkey
- 1 cup cooked brown rice (optional)
- 1 can (14 oz) diced tomatoes
- 1 tsp garlic powder
- Salt and black pepper to taste

Procedure:

1. Preheat oven to 375°F (190°C).
2. Brown ground turkey in a skillet and set aside.
3. In a baking dish, layer cabbage, turkey, rice (if using), and diced tomatoes. Season with garlic powder, salt, and black pepper.
4. Bake for 30 minutes. Serve warm.

Nutritional Info: Approx. 230 calories per serving, 20g protein, 5g fat, 25g carbs (with rice).

Cod with Lemon Dill Sauce

5 mins   15 mins   2

Ingredients:

- 2 cod fillets
- 2 tbsp lemon juice
- 1 tbsp fresh dill, chopped
- Salt and black pepper to taste

Procedure:

1. Preheat oven to 400°F (200°C).
2. Season cod fillets with lemon juice, dill, salt, and black pepper.
3. Place on a lined baking sheet and bake for 15 minutes.
4. Serve with a side of steamed vegetables.

Nutritional Info: Approx. 150 calories per serving, 30g protein, 1g fat, 3g carbs.

Shrimp Stir-Fry with Snow Peas

10 mins   10   2

Ingredients:

- 1 cup shrimp, peeled and deveined
- 1 cup snow peas
- 1 bell pepper, sliced
- 1 tbsp low-sodium soy sauce
- 1 clove garlic, minced

Procedure:

1. Heat a skillet over medium heat and add garlic. Sauté for 1 minute.
2. Add shrimp, snow peas, and bell pepper. Cook for 5-7 minutes.
3. Drizzle with soy sauce and stir well.
4. Serve hot.

Nutritional Info: Approx. 180 calories per serving, 22g protein, 4g fat, 15g carbs.

Zesty Lime Chicken with Cilantro Rice

10 mins   20 mins   2

Ingredients:

- 2 chicken breasts
- 2 tbsp lime juice
- 1 cup cooked cilantro rice (optional)
- Salt and black pepper to taste

Procedure:

1. Marinate chicken breasts in lime juice, salt, and black pepper for 5 minutes.
2. Cook in a skillet over medium heat for 10-12 minutes or until cooked through.
3. Serve with cilantro rice.

Nutritional Info: Approx. 200 calories per serving, 28g protein, 3g fat, 15g carbs (with rice).

White Fish with Garlic Butter

5 mins   10 mins   2

Ingredients:

- 2 fillets of white fish (e.g., tilapia or cod)
- 2 cloves garlic, minced
- 2 tbsp lemon juice
- 1 tbsp fresh parsley, chopped
- Salt and black pepper to taste

Procedure:

1. Preheat a skillet over medium heat and add garlic. Sauté for 1 minute.
2. Place the fish fillets in the skillet and cook for 4-5 minutes on each side or until they flake easily.
3. Drizzle with lemon juice and garnish with parsley.
4. Serve immediately.

Nutritional Info: Approx. 170 calories per serving, 30g protein, 2g fat, 4g carbs.

Sweet and Spicy Tofu Skewers

10 mins   15 mins   4

Ingredients:

- 1 block of firm tofu, cut into cubes
- 2 tbsp low-sodium soy sauce
- 1 tbsp honey
- 1 tsp chili flakes
- Bell pepper and onion chunks for skewers

Procedure:

1. Marinate tofu cubes in soy sauce, honey, and chili flakes for 5 minutes.
2. Thread tofu, bell pepper, and onion onto skewers.
3. Grill over medium heat for 10-15 minutes, turning occasionally.
4. Serve hot.

Nutritional Info: Approx. 150 calories per serving, 10g protein, 4g fat, 12g carbs.

Grilled Asparagus and Lemon Chicken

10 mins   15 mins   2

Ingredients:

- 2 chicken breasts
- 1 bunch asparagus, trimmed
- 2 tbsp lemon juice
- 1 clove garlic, minced
- Salt and black pepper to taste

Procedure:

1. Preheat grill or grill pan over medium heat.
2. Season chicken with lemon juice, garlic, salt, and black pepper.
3. Grill chicken for 7-8 minutes on each side. Grill asparagus for 3-4 minutes, turning occasionally.
4. Serve chicken with grilled asparagus on the side.

Nutritional Info: Approx. 220 calories per serving, 30g protein, 4g fat, 8g carbs

Spicy Black Bean Chili

10 mins   20 mins   4

Ingredients:

- 2 cans (15 oz each) black beans, drained and rinsed
- 1 onion, chopped
- 1 bell pepper, diced
- 1 can (14 oz) diced tomatoes
- 1 tsp chili powder
- ½ tsp cumin
- Salt and black pepper to taste

Procedure:

1. In a pot, sauté the onion and bell pepper for 5 minutes.
2. Add black beans, tomatoes, chili powder, and cumin. Stir well and simmer for 15 minutes.
3. Season with salt and black pepper before serving.

Nutritional Info: Approx. 180 calories per serving, 8g protein, 1g fat, 35g carbs.

Zucchini Noodles with Pesto

5 mins   5 mins   2

Ingredients:

- 2 large zucchinis, spiralized
- 2 tbsp pesto sauce
- 1 tbsp pine nuts (optional)
- Salt and black pepper to taste

Procedure:

1. In a skillet over medium heat, sauté zucchini noodles for 2-3 minutes.
2. Remove from heat and mix with pesto sauce.
3. Garnish with pine nuts and season with salt and black pepper. Serve warm.

Nutritional Info: Approx. 150 calories per serving, 5g protein, 8g fat, 12g carbs.

Quinoa-Stuffed Bell Peppers

10 mins   25 mins   4

Ingredients:

- 4 bell peppers, halved and seeded
- 1 cup cooked quinoa
- 1 cup black beans, drained and rinsed
- ½ cup corn kernels
- 1 tsp cumin
- Salt and black pepper to taste

Procedure:

1. Preheat oven to 375°F (190°C).
2. Mix quinoa, black beans, corn, cumin, salt, and black pepper in a bowl.
3. Stuff bell peppers with the mixture and place them in a baking dish.
4. Bake for 25 minutes. Serve hot.

Nutritional Info: Approx. 200 calories per serving, 8g protein, 3g fat, 35g carbs.

Chicken and Green Bean Stir-Fry

10 mins 10 2

Ingredients:

- 2 chicken breasts, sliced thinly
- 1 cup green beans, trimmed
- 1 clove garlic, minced
- 2 tbsp low-sodium soy sauce
- Salt and black pepper to taste

Procedure:

1. In a skillet over medium heat, sauté garlic for 1 minute.
2. Add chicken and cook for 5 minutes or until no longer pink.
3. Add green beans and soy sauce, cooking for another 3-4 minutes.
4. Season with salt and black pepper. Serve hot.

Nutritional Info: Approx. 220 calories per serving, 30g protein, 3g fat, 10g carbs.

Butternut Squash Soup

10 mins 30 mins 4

Ingredients:

- 1 medium butternut squash, peeled and cubed
- 1 onion, chopped
- 2 cups vegetable broth
- 1 tsp ground cinnamon
- Salt and black pepper to taste

Procedure:

1. In a pot, sauté the onion for 5 minutes.
2. Add butternut squash and vegetable broth. Bring to a boil, then simmer for 20 minutes until squash is tender.
3. Blend until smooth and season with cinnamon, salt, and black pepper.
4. Serve warm.

Nutritional Info: Approx. 140 calories per serving, 2g protein, 1g fat, 30g carbs.

Garlic Lemon Salmon

5 mins   15 mins   2

Ingredients:

- 2 salmon fillets
- 2 tbsp lemon juice
- 2 cloves garlic, minced
- Salt and black pepper to taste
- Fresh dill for garnish (optional)

Procedure:

1. Preheat oven to 400°F (200°C).
2. Place salmon fillets on a baking sheet and season with lemon juice, garlic, salt, and black pepper.
3. Bake for 12-15 minutes or until salmon is cooked through.
4. Garnish with dill and serve with a side of vegetables.

Nutritional Info: Approx. 250 calories per serving, 25g protein, 15g fat, 1g carbs.

Spaghetti Squash with Marinara and Veggies

10 mins   25 mins   2

Ingredients:

- 1 small spaghetti squash
- 1 cup marinara sauce (low-sodium)
- 1 cup diced zucchini
- 1 cup diced mushrooms
- 1 tsp Italian seasoning

Procedure:

1. Preheat oven to 400°F. Cut spaghetti squash in half, scoop out seeds, and bake cut-side down for 25 minutes.
2. Scrape out the "spaghetti" strands, then toss with marinara sauce, zucchini, mushrooms, and Italian seasoning. Serve warm.

Nutritional Info: Approx. 130 calories, 5g protein, 1g fat, 25g carbs.

Stuffed Cabbage Rolls with Tomato Sauce

15 mins   30 mins   4

Ingredients:

- 8 large cabbage leaves
- 1 cup cooked brown rice
- 1 cup diced tomatoes
- 1/2 cup diced carrots
- 1 tsp garlic, minced
- 1 tsp paprika

Procedure:

1. Blanch cabbage leaves in boiling water for 1-2 minutes until softened.
2. In a bowl, mix rice, tomatoes, carrots, garlic, and paprika.
3. Place a spoonful of the mixture in each cabbage leaf, roll up, and place in a baking dish.
4. Bake at 375°F for 30 minutes. Serve with extra tomato sauce if desired.

Nutritional Info: Approx. 150 calories, 4g protein, 1g fat, 30g carbs.

Roasted Vegetable and Chickpea Bowl

10 mins   20 mins   2

Ingredients:

- 1 cup cauliflower florets
- 1 cup diced butternut squash
- 1 cup cherry tomatoes
- 1 can (15 oz) chickpeas, drained and rinsed
- 1 tsp cumin
- Salt and pepper to taste

Procedure:

1. Preheat oven to 400°F. Toss cauliflower, squash, tomatoes, and chickpeas with cumin, salt, and pepper.
2. Spread on a baking sheet and roast for 20 minutes or until vegetables are tender.

Nutritional Info: Approx. 180 calories, 6g protein, 2g fat, 35g carbs.

Zucchini and Mushroom Stir-Fry

 5 mins 10 mins 2

Ingredients:

- 2 zucchinis, sliced
- 1 cup sliced mushrooms
- 1 red bell pepper, sliced
- 1 tbsp low-sodium soy sauce
- 1 tsp sesame seeds (optional)

Procedure:

1. Heat a non-stick skillet over medium-high heat. Add zucchini, mushrooms, and bell pepper.
2. Stir-fry for 8-10 minutes, adding soy sauce in the last 2 minutes. Top with sesame seeds if desired.

Nutritional Info: Approx. 120 calories, 4g protein, 1g fat, 18g carbs.

Broccoli and Cauliflower "Mac" and Cheese

 10 mins 15 mins 2

Ingredients:

- 1 cup broccoli florets
- 1 cup cauliflower florets
- 1/4 cup nutritional yeast
- 1/4 cup unsweetened almond milk
- 1/2 tsp garlic powder
- Salt and black pepper to taste

Procedure:

1. Steam broccoli and cauliflower until tender, about 10 minutes.
2. In a small bowl, mix nutritional yeast, almond milk, garlic powder, salt, and pepper to make a "cheesy" sauce.
3. Pour sauce over the vegetables and mix until coated. Serve warm.

Nutritional Info: Approx. 100 calories, 6g protein, 2g fat, 14g carbs.

Chapter 4
Snacks and Sides

Spicy Roasted Chickpeas

 5 mins   25 mins   4

Ingredients:

- 1 can (15 oz) chickpeas, drained and rinsed
- 1 tsp paprika
- ½ tsp cayenne pepper
- Salt to taste
- Cooking spray

Procedure:

1. Preheat oven to 400°F (200°C).
2. Pat chickpeas dry and spread them on a baking sheet. Spray with cooking spray.
3. Sprinkle paprika, cayenne pepper, and salt over the chickpeas.
4. Roast for 25 minutes or until crispy, shaking the pan halfway through.

Nutritional Info: Approx. 120 calories per serving, 5g protein, 2g fat, 20g carbs.

Fresh Apple Cider Vinegar Slaw

10 *mins*   0 *mins*   4

Ingredients:

- 2 cups shredded cabbage
- 1 cup shredded carrots
- ¼ cup apple cider vinegar
- 1 tbsp honey (optional)
- Salt and black pepper to taste

Procedure:

1. In a large bowl, combine shredded cabbage and carrots.
2. Pour apple cider vinegar over the mixture and add honey if using.
3. Season with salt and black pepper and toss to coat.
4. Chill for 15 minutes before serving.

Nutritional Info: Approx. 70 calories per serving, 1g protein, 0.5g fat, 16g carbs

Simple Guacamole with Crunchy Veggies

5 *mins*   0 *mins*   2

Ingredients:

- 1 avocado, mashed
- 1 tomato, diced
- 1 tbsp lime juice
- Salt and black pepper to taste
- Carrot and celery sticks for serving

Procedure:

1. Mix mashed avocado, diced tomato, and lime juice in a bowl.
2. Season with salt and black pepper.
3. Serve with carrot and celery sticks for dipping.

Nutritional Info: Approx. 160 calories per serving, 3g protein, 12g fat, 15g carbs.

Baked Kale Chips

5 mins   15 mins   2

Ingredients:

- 2 cups kale leaves, stems removed
- 1 tbsp olive oil
- ½ tsp sea salt

Procedure:

1. Preheat oven to 350°F (175°C).
2. Toss kale leaves with olive oil and sprinkle with sea salt.
3. Spread on a baking sheet and bake for 10-15 minutes or until crispy.
4. Let cool before serving.

Nutritional Info: Approx. 80 calories per serving, 3g protein, 4g fat, 10g carbs.

Roasted Red Pepper Hummus

10 mins   mins   4

Ingredients:

- 1 can (15 oz) chickpeas, drained and rinsed
- 1 roasted red pepper
- 2 tbsp tahini
- 2 tbsp lemon juice
- 1 garlic clove
- Salt to taste

Procedure:

1. Blend chickpeas, roasted red pepper, tahini, lemon juice, and garlic in a food processor until smooth.
2. Season with salt and blend again.
3. Serve with pita bread or vegetable sticks.

Nutritional Info: Approx. 110 calories per serving, 5g protein, 4g fat, 15g carbs

Cucumber Dill Dip

5 mins   0 mins   2

Ingredients:

- 1 cup Greek yogurt (non-fat)
- 1 cucumber, grated and drained
- 1 tbsp fresh dill, chopped
- 1 tsp lemon juice
- Salt and black pepper to taste

Procedure:

1. In a bowl, mix Greek yogurt, grated cucumber, dill, and lemon juice.
2. Season with salt and black pepper.
3. Serve chilled with vegetable sticks or crackers.

Nutritional Info: Approx. 80 calories per serving, 10g protein, 0.5g fat, 8g carbs.

Pickled Vegetables

10 mins   0 mins   4

Ingredients:

- 1 cup sliced carrots
- 1 cup sliced cucumbers
- 1 cup cauliflower florets
- 1 cup white vinegar
- 1 tbsp sugar (optional)
- 1 tbsp salt

Procedure:

1. Combine vinegar, sugar (if using), and salt in a jar.
2. Add vegetables to the jar and press down so they are fully submerged.
3. Seal the jar and refrigerate for at least 2 hours before serving.

Nutritional Info: Approx. 50 calories per serving, 2g protein, 0g fat, 12g carbs.

Watermelon and Mint Salad

5 mins   0 mins   2

Ingredients:

- 2 cups cubed watermelon
- 2 tbsp fresh mint leaves, chopped
- 1 tbsp lime juice

Procedure:

1. Combine watermelon and mint in a bowl.
2. Drizzle with lime juice and toss gently.
3. Serve chilled.

Nutritional Info: Approx. 60 calories per serving, 1g protein, 0g fat, 15g carbs.

Spicy Edamame

5 mins   5 mins   2

Ingredients:

- 1 cup edamame (in pods)
- 1 tsp chili flakes
- 1 tsp low-sodium soy sauce

Procedure:

1. Boil edamame in salted water for 5 minutes. Drain.
2. Toss with soy sauce and chili flakes.
3. Serve warm.

Nutritional Info: Approx. 100 calories per serving, 9g protein, 3g fat, 10g carbs.

Steamed Artichoke with Lemon Dip

 5 mins 25 2

Ingredients:

- 2 whole artichokes
- 1 tbsp lemon juice
- 2 tbsp Greek yogurt (non-fat)
- Salt to taste

Procedure:

1. Steam artichokes for 25 minutes or until leaves are tender.
2. Mix Greek yogurt and lemon juice for the dip.
3. Serve artichokes with lemon dip.

Nutritional Info: Approx. 80 calories per serving, 5g protein, 0.5g fat, 18g carbs.

Air-Fried Sweet Potato Wedges

 5 mins 15 mins 2

Ingredients:

- 1 large sweet potato, cut into wedges
- 1 tbsp olive oil
- ½ tsp paprika
- Salt to taste

Procedure:

1. Preheat air fryer to 400°F (200°C).
2. Toss sweet potato wedges with olive oil, paprika, and salt.
3. Air-fry for 15 minutes, shaking halfway through.
4. Serve hot.

Nutritional Info: Approx. 150 calories per serving, 2g protein, 4g fat, 30g carbs.

Roasted Brussels Sprouts with Balsamic

 5 mins   20 mins   2

Ingredients:

- 2 cups Brussels sprouts, halved
- 1 tbsp balsamic vinegar
- Salt and black pepper to taste

Procedure:

1. Preheat oven to 400°F (200°C).
2. Toss Brussels sprouts with balsamic vinegar, salt, and black pepper.
3. Roast for 20 minutes, flipping halfway through.
4. Serve warm

Nutritional Info: Approx. 90 calories per serving, 4g protein, 1g fat, 18g carbs.

Grilled Corn with Paprika

 5 mins   10 mins   2

Ingredients:

- 2 ears of corn, husked
- 1 tsp paprika
- 1 tbsp lime juice

Procedure:

1. Grill corn over medium heat for 10 minutes, turning occasionally.
2. Sprinkle with paprika and drizzle with lime juice.
3. Serve immediately.

Nutritional Info: Approx. 100 calories per serving, 3g protein, 1g fat, 22g carbs.

Tomato and Basil Bruschetta

10 *mins*   5 *mins*   4

Ingredients:

- 4 slices whole-grain bread (optional)
- 2 tomatoes, diced
- 2 tbsp fresh basil, chopped
- 1 tbsp balsamic vinegar
- Salt and black pepper to taste

Procedure:

1. Toast bread slices if using.
2. Mix diced tomatoes, basil, balsamic vinegar, salt, and black pepper.
3. Spoon the tomato mixture onto toasted bread.
4. Serve immediately.

Nutritional Info: Approx. 80 calories per serving, 3g protein, 1g fat, 15g carbs (without bread).

Chapter 5

Desserts Without the Guilt

Baked Cinnamon Apples

5 mins 　　　　20 mins 　　　　　2

Ingredients:

- 2 large apples, cored and sliced
- 1 tsp cinnamon
- 1 tbsp water
- 1 tsp vanilla extract (optional)

Procedure:

1. Preheat oven to 375°F (190°C).
2. Place apple slices in a baking dish and sprinkle with cinnamon.
3. Add water and vanilla extract if using.
4. Bake for 20 minutes or until apples are tender.
5. Serve warm.

Nutritional Info: Approx. 90 calories per serving, 1g protein, 0g fat, 24g carbs.

Berry Parfait with Zero Point Yogurt

 5 mins   0 mins   2

Ingredients:

- 1 cup non-fat Greek yogurt
- 1 cup mixed berries (strawberries, blueberries, raspberries)
- 1 tbsp honey (optional)

Procedure:

1. In a serving glass, layer Greek yogurt and mixed berries.
2. Drizzle with honey if desired.
3. Repeat the layers and serve chilled.

Nutritional Info: Approx. 100 calories per serving, 10g protein, 0g fat, 20g carbs.

Fruity Sorbet

 10 mins   0 mins   4

Ingredients:

- 2 cups frozen mango chunks
- 1 cup frozen pineapple chunks
- 2 tbsp lime juice

Procedure:

1. Blend frozen mango, pineapple, and lime juice in a food processor until smooth.
2. Transfer to a container and freeze for 2 hours.
3. Scoop and serve chilled.

Nutritional Info: Approx. 80 calories per serving, 1g protein, 0g fat, 20g carbs.

Chocolate Banana Bites

 10 mins   0 mins   4

Ingredients:

- 2 bananas, sliced
- 2 tbsp cocoa powder
- 1 tbsp water

Procedure:

1. Mix cocoa powder and water to create a smooth paste.
2. Dip banana slices into the cocoa mixture and place on a parchment-lined tray.
3. Freeze for 1 hour and serve.

Nutritional Info: Approx. 70 calories per serving, 1g protein, 0.5g fat, 18g carbs.

Mango Pineapple Popsicles

 5 mins   0 mins   4

Ingredients:

- 1 cup mango chunks
- 1 cup pineapple chunks
- ½ cup water

Procedure:

1. Blend mango, pineapple, and water until smooth.
2. Pour the mixture into popsicle molds and freeze for 4 hours.
3. Serve frozen.

Nutritional Info: Approx. 60 calories per serving, 0.5g protein, 0g fat, 15g carbs.

Chia Seed Pudding with Blueberries

5 mins   0 mins   2

Ingredients:

- 2 tbsp chia seeds
- 1 cup unsweetened almond milk
- ½ cup fresh blueberries
- 1 tsp vanilla extract (optional)

Procedure:

1. Mix chia seeds, almond milk, and vanilla extract in a bowl.
2. Stir well, cover, and refrigerate overnight.
3. Top with fresh blueberries before serving.

Nutritional Info: Approx. 100 calories per serving, 3g protein, 4g fat, 15g carbs.

Zero Point Lemon Mousse

10 mins   0 mins   2

Ingredients:

- 1 cup non-fat Greek yogurt
- 2 tbsp lemon juice
- 1 tbsp lemon zest
- Sweetener of choice (optional)

Procedure:

1. Mix Greek yogurt, lemon juice, lemon zest, and sweetener in a bowl.
2. Spoon into serving cups and refrigerate for 1 hour.
3. Serve chilled with a garnish of lemon zest.

Nutritional Info: Approx. 80 calories per serving, 10g protein, 0g fat, 10g carbs.

Poached Pears with Vanilla

5 mins 20 2

Ingredients:

- 2 pears, peeled and halved
- 2 cups water
- 1 tsp vanilla extract
- 1 tbsp honey (optional)

Procedure:

1. Bring water and vanilla extract to a simmer in a saucepan.
2. Add pears and poach for 20 minutes or until tender.
3. Drizzle with honey if desired and serve warm or chilled.

Nutritional Info: Approx. 100 calories per serving, 1g protein, 0g fat, 26g carbs.

Apple and Cinnamon Compote

5 mins 15 mins 2

Ingredients:

- 2 apples, peeled and diced
- 1 tsp cinnamon
- 2 tbsp water

Procedure:

1. Combine apples, cinnamon, and water in a saucepan over medium heat.
2. Cook for 15 minutes, stirring occasionally, until apples are soft.
3. Serve warm as a dessert or topping

Nutritional Info: Approx. 80 calories per serving, 1g protein, 0g fat, 22g carbs.

Chapter 6

Quick and Easy Family Meals

Family-Friendly One-Pot Dishes

10 mins

30 mins

4

Ingredients:

- 1 lb chicken breast, diced
- 2 cups mixed vegetables (carrots, peas, corn)
- 1 cup low-sodium chicken broth
- 1 tsp garlic powder
- Salt and black pepper to taste

Procedure:

1. In a large pot, sauté chicken until cooked through.
2. Add mixed vegetables, chicken broth, garlic powder, salt, and black pepper.
3. Simmer for 15-20 minutes and serve hot.

Nutritional Info: Approx. 250 calories per serving, 30g protein, 4g fat, 20g carbs.

Zero Point Stir-Fry with Seasonal Vegetables

5 mins   10 mins   2

Ingredients:

- 2 cups seasonal vegetables (broccoli, bell peppers, carrots)
- 1 tbsp low-sodium soy sauce
- 1 tsp ginger, grated
- Salt and black pepper to taste

Procedure:

1. Heat a wok or large skillet over medium-high heat.
2. Add vegetables and stir-fry for 5-7 minutes.
3. Drizzle with soy sauce and sprinkle ginger.
4. Serve immediately.

Nutritional Info: Approx. 90 calories per serving, 3g protein, 1g fat, 18g carbs

Budget Meals for Under $10

5 mins   20 mins   4

Ingredients:

- 2 cups cooked rice
- 1 can (15 oz) black beans, drained and rinsed
- 1 cup corn kernels
- 1 cup salsa
- Fresh cilantro for garnish

Procedure:

1. Combine cooked rice, black beans, corn, and salsa in a skillet over medium heat.
2. Cook for 10 minutes, stirring occasionally.
3. Garnish with cilantro and serve.

Nutritional Info: Approx. 220 calories per serving, 7g protein, 2g fat, 45g carbs.

Turkey Chili with Beans

10 mins   30 mins   4

Ingredients:

- 1 lb ground turkey
- 1 can (15 oz) kidney beans, drained and rinsed
- 1 can (14 oz) diced tomatoes
- 1 tbsp chili powder
- Salt and black pepper to taste

Procedure:

1. Brown ground turkey in a pot over medium heat.
2. Add kidney beans, diced tomatoes, chili powder, salt, and black pepper.
3. Simmer for 20-25 minutes. Serve hot.

Nutritional Info: Approx. 250 calories per serving, 25g protein, 5g fat, 30g carbs.

Lemon Garlic Shrimp Pasta

5 mins   10 mins   2

Ingredients:

- 1 cup whole wheat spaghetti (cooked)
- 1 cup shrimp, peeled and deveined
- 2 cloves garlic, minced
- 2 tbsp lemon juice
- Fresh parsley for garnish

Procedure:

1. In a skillet, sauté garlic for 1 minute.
2. Add shrimp and cook for 2-3 minutes until pink.
3. Toss with cooked spaghetti and lemon juice.
4. Garnish with parsley and serve.

Nutritional Info: Approx. 300 calories per serving, 25g protein, 4g fat, 50g carbs.

Chicken and Broccoli Casserole

 10 mins   25 mins   4

Ingredients:

- 2 cups cooked chicken breast, shredded
- 2 cups broccoli florets
- 1 cup low-fat Greek yogurt
- ½ cup shredded cheddar cheese (optional)
- Salt and black pepper to taste

Procedure:

1. Preheat oven to 375°F (190°C).
2. In a baking dish, mix chicken, broccoli, Greek yogurt, and salt and black pepper.
3. Top with cheddar cheese if using and bake for 20-25 minutes.
4. Serve hot.

Nutritional Info: Approx. 200 calories per serving, 30g protein, 4g fat, 10g carbs.

Zoodle Spaghetti with Turkey Meat Sauce

 10 mins   15 mins   2

Ingredients:

- 2 large zucchinis, spiralized
- 1 lb ground turkey
- 1 cup marinara sauce
- 1 tsp Italian seasoning

Procedure:

1. Cook ground turkey in a skillet until no longer pink. Add marinara sauce and Italian seasoning.
2. Sauté zoodles in a separate pan for 3-4 minutes.
3. Top zoodles with turkey meat sauce and serve.

Nutritional Info: Approx. 250 calories per serving, 35g protein, 5g fat, 15g carbs.

Sweet Potato Shepherd's Pie

15 *mins*   30   4

Ingredients:

- 2 large sweet potatoes, peeled and mashed
- 1 lb ground turkey or chicken
- 1 cup mixed vegetables (peas, carrots, corn)
- Salt and black pepper to taste

Procedure:

1. Preheat oven to 375°F (190°C).
2. Cook ground turkey in a skillet and add mixed vegetables.
3. Transfer to a baking dish and spread mashed sweet potatoes on top.
4. Bake for 25-30 minutes. Serve hot.

Nutritional Info: Approx. 280 calories per serving, 20g protein, 6g fat, 45g carbs.

Vegetable Paella

10 *mins*   25 *mins*   4

Ingredients:

- 1 cup brown rice
- 1 red bell pepper, diced
- 1 cup green beans, trimmed
- 1 tsp smoked paprika
- 2 cups vegetable broth

Procedure:

1. Sauté bell pepper and green beans in a large skillet.
2. Add rice, smoked paprika, and vegetable broth.
3. Simmer for 20-25 minutes or until rice is tender.
4. Serve warm.

Nutritional Info: Approx. 180 calories per serving, 5g protein, 2g fat, 35g carbs.

Zero Point Sloppy Joes

10 *mins*   20   4

Ingredients:

- 1 lb lean ground turkey
- 1 can (14 oz) tomato sauce
- 1 tbsp Worcestershire sauce
- 1 tsp garlic powder
- Salt and black pepper to taste

Procedure:

1. Cook ground turkey in a skillet until browned.
2. Add tomato sauce, Worcestershire sauce, garlic powder, salt, and black pepper.
3. Simmer for 10 minutes and serve over whole wheat buns or lettuce wraps.

Nutritional Info: Approx. 200 calories per serving, 25g protein, 3g fat, 15g carbs.

Grilled Chicken and Pineapple Bowls

10 *mins*   10 *mins*   2

Ingredients:

- 2 chicken breasts, grilled and sliced
- 1 cup pineapple chunks
- 1 cup cooked brown rice
- 1 tbsp teriyaki sauce

Procedure:

1. Grill chicken breasts and slice them.
2. In a bowl, combine cooked brown rice, grilled chicken, and pineapple chunks.
3. Drizzle with teriyaki sauce and serve.

Nutritional Info: Approx. 250 calories per serving, 30g protein, 3g fat, 35g carbs

Spaghetti Squash Marinara

 10 mins   30 mins   2

Ingredients:

- 1 spaghetti squash, halved and seeded
- 1 cup marinara sauce
- 1 tbsp Parmesan cheese (optional)

Procedure:

1. Preheat oven to 400°F (200°C) and roast squash for 30 minutes.
2. Scrape squash strands with a fork and mix with marinara sauce.
3. Top with Parmesan cheese if desired and serve.

Nutritional Info: Approx. 150 calories per serving, 5g protein, 1g fat, 35g carbs.

BBQ Cauliflower Bites

5 mins   20 mins   4

Ingredients:

- 1 head cauliflower, cut into florets
- ½ cup BBQ sauce
- Cooking spray

Procedure:

1. Preheat oven to 425°F (220°C).
2. Toss cauliflower florets with BBQ sauce.
3. Spread on a baking sheet and bake for 20 minutes.
4. Serve warm.

Nutritional Info: Approx. 100 calories per serving, 2g protein, 1g fat, 22g carbs.

Thai-Inspired Chicken Soup

10 *mins*

20

4

Ingredients:

- 2 chicken breasts, shredded
- 1 can (14 oz) coconut milk (light)
- 2 cups chicken broth
- 1 tbsp ginger, grated
- 1 tbsp lime juice

Procedure:

1. In a pot, combine chicken broth, coconut milk, ginger, and shredded chicken.
2. Simmer for 15 minutes and add lime juice.
3. Serve warm.

Nutritional Info: Approx. 180 calories per serving, 20g protein, 7g fat, 10g carbs.

Butternut Squash Mac and Cheese

10 *mins*

20 *mins*

4

Ingredients:

- 2 cups cooked whole wheat pasta
- 1 cup butternut squash puree
- ½ cup low-fat cheddar cheese
- Salt and black pepper to taste

Procedure:

1. In a pot, combine cooked pasta, butternut squash puree, and cheddar cheese.
2. Stir over low heat until cheese is melted and creamy.
3. Season with salt and black pepper. Serve hot.

Nutritional Info: Approx. 250 calories per serving, 12g protein, 4g fat, 40g carbs.

Chapter 7

Bonuses

Thank you for choosing *Super Easy Zero Point Weight Loss Cookbook*! To enhance your journey, here are three exclusive guides designed to support your health and wellness.

Here is what you'll disconer:

- Mindful Eating & Stress Management
- Home Workout Routine
- Sleep Optimization

Scan the QR code below to download your bonuses! Enjoy the journey to a healthier you.

Chapter 8

60-Day Meal Plan for Fast and Sustainable Weight Loss

Week 1 Meal Plan

Breakfasts

1. Savory Zero Point Omelet with Vegetables
2. Overnight Chia Seed Pudding
3. Berry Smoothie Bowl
4. Zero Point Banana Pancakes
5. Oatmeal with Apple and Cinnamon
6. Spiced Pear Compote
7. Veggie Breakfast Burrito

Lunches

1. Grilled Chicken and Spinach Salad
2. Mediterranean Chickpea Salad
3. Zero Point Lentil Curry
4. Cucumber and Tomato Salad with Basil
5. Roasted Beet Salad with Arugula
6. Shrimp and Avocado Salad
7. Spicy Black Bean Chili

Dinners

1. Baked Lemon Herb Fish with Steamed Vegetables
2. Turkey Meatballs with Marinara Sauce
3. Herb-Roasted Chicken Thighs
4. Grilled Zucchini Lasagna
5. Zero Point Ratatouille
6. Spaghetti Squash Primavera
7. Chicken and Green Bean Stir-Fry

Snacks

1. Spicy Roasted Chickpeas
2. Simple Guacamole with Crunchy Veggies
3. Air-Fried Sweet Potato Wedges
4. Roasted Red Pepper Hummus
5. Watermelon and Mint Salad
6. Cucumber Dill Dip
7. Baked Kale Chips

Week 1 Shopping List

- Produce: 2 large zucchinis, 1 head broccoli, 1 bunch spinach, 4 bell peppers, cherry tomatoes, 2 cucumbers, 1 bag mixed greens, 1 bunch asparagus, 1 bunch cilantro, 2 lemons, 1 lime, 1 head garlic, 2 onions, 4 sweet potatoes, 1 small butternut squash, 2 apples, 1 bunch bananas, 1 small watermelon, fresh dill, basil leaves, 1 pint blueberries, 1 bag mixed berries, 1 small pineapple, 1 avocado, 1 bag baby carrots.

- Protein: 6 chicken breasts, 1 lb ground turkey, 2 lbs white fish fillets, 1 bag shrimp, 1 dozen eggs.
- Grains: 1 box quick oats, 1 bag brown rice, 1 box whole wheat spaghetti, 1 bag quinoa.
- Canned/Bottled: 2 cans chickpeas, 1 can black beans, 1 can kidney beans, 1 jar low-sodium marinara sauce, 1 can diced tomatoes, 1 jar salsa, balsamic vinegar, apple cider vinegar.
- Dairy: 1 container non-fat Greek yogurt, ricotta cheese (optional), shredded cheddar cheese (optional).
- Spices/Herbs: Cinnamon, paprika, cumin, chili powder, garlic powder, Italian seasoning, ground ginger.
- Miscellaneous: Cooking spray, honey (optional), almond milk, chia seeds.

Week 1 Prep Tips

- Batch Cook: Prepare the zero-point lentil curry and grilled chicken for easy lunch portions.
- Cut Veggies: Chop cucumbers, bell peppers, and carrots for snacks.
- Make Ahead: Prep overnight chia seed pudding the night before.

- Freeze Smoothies: Portion out smoothie ingredients in freezer bags for quick blending.
- Seasoned Proteins: Marinate chicken breasts with lemon juice, garlic, and herbs for dinners later in the week.

Week 2 Meal Plan

Breakfasts

1. Spinach and Tomato Scramble
2. Lemon Ricotta Toast
3. Grilled Pineapple Slices
4. Fresh Fruit Salad with a Twist
5. Breakfast Quinoa Bowl
6. Savory Zero Point Omelet with Vegetables
7. Berry Parfait with Zero Point Yogurt

Lunches

1. Roasted Cauliflower Tacos
2. Turkey Chili with Beans
3. Cabbage Roll Casserole
4. Vegetable Paella
5. Zero Point Sloppy Joes
6. Grilled Chicken and Pineapple Bowls
7. Chicken Lettuce Wraps

Dinners

1. Eggplant Parmesan with Tomato Sauce

2. Balsamic-Glazed Chicken Breast
3. Cod with Lemon Dill Sauce
4. Zero Point Minestrone Soup
5. Lentil Shepherd's Pie
6. Butternut Squash Soup
7. Garlic Lemon Salmon

Snacks

1. Pickled Vegetables
2. Spicy Edamame
3. Tomato and Basil Bruschetta
4. Simple Guacamole with Crunchy Veggies
5. Fresh Apple Cider Vinegar Slaw
6. Chia Seed Pudding with Blueberries
7. Steamed Artichoke with Lemon Dip

Week 2 Shopping List

- Produce: Eggplant, 1 head cauliflower, 1 head cabbage, 1 bag green beans, cherry tomatoes, 2 large sweet potatoes, 4 bell peppers, 1 bunch spinach, arugula, 2 cucumbers, fresh dill, parsley, cilantro, 1 bunch basil leaves, 2 lemons, 2 limes, 1 head garlic, 1 bag carrots, 1 avocado, 1 bag mixed berries, fresh mint.
- Protein: 4 chicken breasts, 1 lb ground turkey, 2 cod fillets, 2 salmon fillets.
- Grains: 1 bag brown rice, 1 box whole wheat spaghetti, 1 pack tortillas, 1 bag quinoa.

- Canned/Bottled: 2 cans kidney beans, 2 cans chickpeas, 1 can black beans, 1 jar low-sodium marinara sauce, 1 can diced tomatoes.
- Dairy: Ricotta cheese (optional), shredded mozzarella cheese (optional).
- Spices/Herbs: Oregano, cumin, smoked paprika, Italian seasoning.
- Miscellaneous: Cooking spray, balsamic vinegar, almond milk, chia seeds, soy sauce.

Week 2 Prep Tips

- Batch Cook: Make turkey chili and vegetable paella for easy reheat meals.
- Make Dressings: Prepare apple cider vinegar slaw dressing and keep it ready.
- Roast Veggies: Roast extra bell peppers and cauliflower for snacks.
- Plan Wraps: Pre-fill lettuce wraps and store in an airtight container for quick lunches.

Week 3 Meal Plan

Breakfasts

1. Overnight Chia Seed Pudding
2. Zero Point Banana Pancakes
3. Savory Zero Point Omelet with Vegetables
4. Berry Smoothie Bowl

5. Lemon Ricotta Toast
6. Oatmeal with Apple and Cinnamon
7. Fresh Fruit Salad with a Twist

Lunches

1. Mediterranean Chickpea Salad
2. Chicken Lettuce Wraps
3. Zero Point Lentil Curry
4. Tuna and White Bean Salad
5. Roasted Beet Salad with Arugula
6. Spicy Black Bean Chili
7. Cucumber and Tomato Salad with Basil

Dinners

1. Herb-Roasted Chicken Thighs
2. Grilled Zucchini Lasagna
3. Eggplant Parmesan with Tomato Sauce
4. Baked Lemon Herb Fish with Steamed Vegetables
5. Lemon-Garlic Chicken Skewers
6. Cod with Lemon Dill Sauce
7. Spaghetti Squash Primavera

Snacks

1. Air-Fried Sweet Potato Wedges
2. Roasted Red Pepper Hummus
3. Pickled Vegetables
4. Tomato and Basil Bruschetta
5. Spicy Roasted Chickpeas
6. Simple Guacamole with Crunchy Veggies
7. Fresh Apple Cider Vinegar Slaw

Week 3 Shopping List

- Produce: 1 head cauliflower, 2 zucchinis, 1 eggplant, cherry tomatoes, 4 sweet potatoes, 1 bunch spinach, 1 head cabbage, arugula, 2 lemons, 2 limes, fresh basil, cilantro, parsley, 1 bunch green onions, 1 bag baby carrots, 1 avocado, mixed berries, 1 pineapple, 2 cucumbers.
- Protein: 4 chicken thighs, 1 lb ground turkey, 2 cod fillets, 1 can tuna, 1 dozen eggs.
- Grains: 1 box whole wheat spaghetti, 1 bag quinoa, 1 box quick oats.
- Canned/Bottled: 1 jar marinara sauce, 1 can chickpeas, 2 cans black beans, 1 can white beans, 1 can kidney beans.
- Dairy: Ricotta cheese (optional), Greek yogurt (non-fat).
- Spices/Herbs: Cinnamon, oregano, smoked paprika, Italian seasoning, cumin.
- Miscellaneous: Cooking spray, almond milk, chia seeds, balsamic vinegar, honey (optional).

Week 3 Prep Tips

- Batch Cook: Prepare a large batch of lentil curry and herb-roasted chicken thighs for reheating.
- Chop Vegetables: Pre-cut cucumbers, carrots, and bell peppers for snacks and salads.

- Overnight Prep: Make chia seed pudding and marinate chicken for meals later in the week.
- Store Smart: Store leafy greens in airtight containers with a paper towel to keep them fresh.

Week 4 Meal Plan

Breakfasts

1. Spinach and Tomato Scramble
2. Lemon Ricotta Toast
3. Overnight Chia Seed Pudding
4. Zero Point Banana Pancakes
5. Oatmeal with Apple and Cinnamon
6. Veggie Breakfast Burrito
7. Berry Parfait with Zero Point Yogurt

Lunches

1. Roasted Cauliflower Tacos
2. Turkey Chili with Beans
3. Vegetable Paella
4. Chicken and Broccoli Casserole
5. Zero Point Sloppy Joes
6. Tuna and White Bean Salad
7. Grilled Chicken and Pineapple Bowls

Dinners

1. Lentil Shepherd's Pie
2. Balsamic-Glazed Chicken Breast
3. Herb-Roasted Chicken Thighs
4. Zero Point Minestrone Soup
5. Garlic Lemon Salmon
6. Shrimp Stir-Fry with Snow Peas
7. Chicken and Green Bean Stir-Fry

Snacks

1. Baked Kale Chips
2. Spicy Edamame
3. Roasted Brussels Sprouts with Balsamic
4. Steamed Artichoke with Lemon Dip
5. Chia Seed Pudding with Blueberries
6. Simple Guacamole with Crunchy Veggies
7. Fresh Apple Cider Vinegar Slaw

Week 4 Shopping List

- Produce: 2 heads cauliflower, 1 bag green beans, cherry tomatoes, 2 sweet potatoes, 1 bunch spinach, 1 head cabbage, arugula, 3 lemons, 2 limes, fresh basil, cilantro, parsley, 1 bunch green onions, baby carrots, 1 avocado, mixed berries, 1 small watermelon, 1 bunch asparagus.
- Protein: 1 lb ground turkey, 2 chicken breasts, 2 salmon fillets, 1 lb shrimp, 1 dozen eggs.
- Grains: 1 bag quinoa, 1 box whole wheat spaghetti, 1 bag brown rice.
- Canned/Bottled: 1 jar marinara sauce, 2 cans black beans, 1 can kidney beans, 1 can chickpeas, 1 can white beans.
- Dairy: Ricotta cheese (optional), Greek yogurt (non-fat).

- Spices/Herbs: Cinnamon, paprika, cumin, garlic powder, chili powder.
- Miscellaneous: Cooking spray, almond milk, chia seeds, soy sauce.

Week 4 Prep Tips

- Batch Cook: Make turkey chili and vegetable paella to last several lunches.
- Meal Prep: Assemble chicken and broccoli casserole to save time during the week.
- Snack Prep: Make roasted Brussels sprouts and kale chips in advance.
- Chill Overnight: Prep chia seed pudding the night before for a quick breakfast.

Week 5 Meal Plan

Breakfasts

1. Savory Zero Point Omelet with Vegetables
2. Overnight Chia Seed Pudding
3. Breakfast Quinoa Bowl
4. Berry Smoothie Bowl
5. Spiced Pear Compote
6. Lemon Ricotta Toast
7. Fresh Fruit Salad with a Twist

Lunches

1. Mediterranean Chickpea Salad
2. Zero Point Lentil Curry
3. Tuna and White Bean Salad

4. Grilled Chicken and Spinach Salad
5. Roasted Beet Salad with Arugula
6. Vegetable Paella
7. Chicken Lettuce Wraps

Dinners

1. Baked Lemon Herb Fish with Steamed Vegetables
2. Spinach-Stuffed Portobello Mushrooms
3. Eggplant Parmesan with Tomato Sauce
4. Herb-Roasted Chicken Thighs
5. Lemon-Garlic Chicken Skewers
6. Butternut Squash Soup
7. Garlic Lemon Salmon

Snacks

1. Spicy Roasted Chickpeas
2. Air-Fried Sweet Potato Wedges
3. Pickled Vegetables
4. Tomato and Basil Bruschetta
5. Simple Guacamole with Crunchy Veggies
6. Steamed Artichoke with Lemon Dip
7. Baked Kale Chips

Week 5 Shopping List

- Produce: 1 head cauliflower, 1 bunch spinach, 1 eggplant, 4 bell peppers, cherry tomatoes, 1 bunch asparagus, 2 zucchinis, 1 bag mixed greens, 1 bunch cilantro, parsley, 2 lemons, 2 limes, fresh dill, basil leaves, 1 pint blueberries, 1 bag mixed berries, 1 pineapple, 1 avocado.

- Protein: 4 chicken thighs, 2 cod fillets, 1 dozen eggs, 1 can tuna, 2 salmon fillets.
- Grains: 1 bag quinoa, 1 box quick oats, 1 box whole wheat spaghetti.
- Canned/Bottled: 1 jar marinara sauce, 2 cans chickpeas, 1 can white beans, 1 can kidney beans.
- Dairy: Ricotta cheese (optional), Greek yogurt (non-fat).
- Spices/Herbs: Cinnamon, paprika, cumin, Italian seasoning, ground ginger.
- Miscellaneous: Cooking spray, almond milk, honey (optional), chia seeds, balsamic vinegar.

Week 5 Prep Tips

- Batch Cook: Prepare lentil curry and herb-roasted chicken thighs for easy reheating.
- Snack Prep: Make roasted chickpeas and kale chips ahead of time.
- Pre-Cut Vegetables: Slice cucumbers, bell peppers, and carrots for easy snacking and salads.
- Overnight Prep: Set up overnight chia pudding and refrigerate for a grab-and-go breakfast.

Week 6 Meal Plan

Breakfasts

1. Oatmeal with Apple and Cinnamon
2. Savory Zero Point Omelet with Vegetables
3. Veggie Breakfast Burrito
4. Berry Parfait with Zero Point Yogurt
5. Grilled Pineapple Slices
6. Overnight Chia Seed Pudding
7. Zero Point Banana Pancakes

Lunches

1. Roasted Cauliflower Tacos
2. Turkey Chili with Beans
3. Cucumber and Tomato Salad with Basil
4. Zero Point Lentil Curry
5. Tuna and White Bean Salad
6. Grilled Chicken and Spinach Salad
7. Vegetable Paella

Dinners

1. Spinach-Stuffed Portobello Mushrooms
2. Balsamic-Glazed Chicken Breast
3. Herb-Roasted Chicken Thighs
4. Eggplant Parmesan with Tomato Sauce
5. Zero Point Minestrone Soup
6. Shrimp Stir-Fry with Snow Peas
7. Chicken and Green Bean Stir-Fry

Snacks

1. Roasted Red Pepper Hummus
2. Pickled Vegetables
3. Spicy Edamame
4. Steamed Artichoke with Lemon Dip
5. Cucumber Dill Dip
6. Tomato and Basil Bruschetta
7. Watermelon and Mint Salad

Week 6 Shopping List

- Produce: 2 zucchinis, 1 head cauliflower, 1 head cabbage, cherry tomatoes, 2 sweet potatoes, 1 bunch spinach, arugula, 1 bunch cilantro, 2 lemons, 2 limes, fresh dill, 1 pint blueberries, 1 bag mixed berries, 1 watermelon, 1 avocado, 1 bunch green beans.
- Protein: 1 lb ground turkey, 4 chicken thighs, 2 salmon fillets, 1 lb shrimp, 1 dozen eggs.
- Grains: 1 bag quinoa, 1 box whole wheat spaghetti, 1 box quick oats.
- Canned/Bottled: 1 jar marinara sauce, 2 cans chickpeas, 1 can white beans, 2 cans black beans.
- Dairy: Ricotta cheese (optional), Greek yogurt (non-fat).
- Spices/Herbs: Cinnamon, cumin, garlic powder, chili powder.
- Miscellaneous: Cooking spray, almond milk, chia seeds, soy sauce.

Week 6 Prep Tips

- Batch Cook: Make turkey chili and lentil curry for meal prepping.

- Pre-Cut Veggies: Chop vegetables for salads and wraps.
- Snack Prep: Prepare edamame and artichoke in advance.
- Overnight Prep: Make chia pudding and set up overnight oats for easy breakfasts.

Week 7 Meal Plan

Breakfasts

1. Fresh Fruit Salad with a Twist
2. Lemon Ricotta Toast
3. Savory Zero Point Omelet with Vegetables
4. Overnight Chia Seed Pudding
5. Berry Smoothie Bowl
6. Spiced Pear Compote
7. Oatmeal with Apple and Cinnamon

Lunches

1. Mediterranean Chickpea Salad
2. Grilled Chicken and Pineapple Bowls
3. Zero Point Lentil Curry
4. Cucumber and Tomato Salad with Basil
5. Roasted Beet Salad with Arugula
6. Tuna and White Bean Salad
7. Vegetable Paella

Dinners

1. Herb-Roasted Chicken Thighs

2. Spinach-Stuffed Portobello Mushrooms
3. Eggplant Parmesan with Tomato Sauce
4. Baked Lemon Herb Fish with Steamed Vegetables
5. Lemon-Garlic Chicken Skewers
6. Cod with Lemon Dill Sauce
7. Garlic Lemon Salmon

Snacks

1. Simple Guacamole with Crunchy Veggies
2. Air-Fried Sweet Potato Wedges
3. Tomato and Basil Bruschetta
4. Roasted Red Pepper Hummus
5. Pickled Vegetables
6. Watermelon and Mint Salad
7. Cucumber Dill Dip

Week 7 Shopping List

- Produce: 1 head cauliflower, 2 zucchinis, 1 eggplant, cherry tomatoes, 4 sweet potatoes, 1 bunch spinach, 1 head cabbage, arugula, 3 lemons, 2 limes, fresh dill, basil leaves, 1 pint blueberries, 1 bag mixed berries, 1 small watermelon, 1 bunch asparagus.
- Protein: 4 chicken thighs, 2 cod fillets, 1 dozen eggs, 1 can tuna, 2 salmon fillets.
- Grains: 1 bag quinoa, 1 box whole wheat spaghetti, 1 box quick oats.

- Canned/Bottled: 1 jar marinara sauce, 2 cans chickpeas, 1 can white beans.
- Dairy: Ricotta cheese (optional), Greek yogurt (non-fat).
- Spices/Herbs: Cinnamon, paprika, cumin, Italian seasoning, ground ginger.
- Miscellaneous: Cooking spray, almond milk, honey (optional), chia seeds, balsamic vinegar.

Week 7 Prep Tips

- Batch Cook: Prepare lentil curry and roasted chicken thighs for reheating.
- Chop Vegetables: Pre-slice cucumbers, bell peppers, and carrots for snacks and salads.
- Make Overnight Meals: Prepare chia pudding and store overnight.
- Roast Snacks: Make roasted chickpeas and sweet potato wedges for snacks.

Week 8 Meal Plan

Breakfasts

1. Savory Zero Point Omelet with Vegetables
2. Overnight Chia Seed Pudding
3. Berry Smoothie Bowl
4. Zero Point Banana Pancakes
5. Lemon Ricotta Toast

6. Grilled Pineapple Slices
7. Veggie Breakfast Burrito

Lunches

1. Chicken Lettuce Wraps
2. Tuna and White Bean Salad
3. Zero Point Lentil Curry
4. Mediterranean Chickpea Salad
5. Cucumber and Tomato Salad with Basil
6. Vegetable Paella
7. Grilled Chicken and Spinach Salad

Dinners

1. Balsamic-Glazed Chicken Breast
2. Spinach-Stuffed Portobello Mushrooms
3. Eggplant Parmesan with Tomato Sauce
4. Lentil Shepherd's Pie
5. Garlic Lemon Salmon
6. Butternut Squash Soup
7. Lemon-Garlic Chicken Skewers

Snacks

1. Spicy Roasted Chickpeas
2. Air-Fried Sweet Potato Wedges
3. Simple Guacamole with Crunchy Veggies
4. Tomato and Basil Bruschetta
5. Pickled Vegetables
6. Roasted Brussels Sprouts with Balsamic
7. Fresh Apple Cider Vinegar Slaw

Week 8 Shopping List

- Produce: 2 zucchinis, 1 head cauliflower, 1 eggplant, cherry tomatoes, 4 sweet potatoes, 1 bunch spinach, 1 head cabbage, arugula, 3 lemons, 2 limes, fresh dill, 1 pint blueberries, 1 bag mixed berries, 1 small watermelon, 1 bunch green beans, basil leaves.
- Protein: 4 chicken thighs, 2 cod fillets, 1 dozen eggs, 1 can tuna, 2 salmon fillets.
- Grains: 1 bag quinoa, 1 box whole wheat spaghetti, 1 box quick oats.
- Canned/Bottled: 1 jar marinara sauce, 2 cans chickpeas, 1 can white beans.
- Dairy: Ricotta cheese (optional), Greek yogurt (non-fat).
- Spices/Herbs: Cinnamon, cumin, garlic powder, Italian seasoning, smoked paprika.
- Miscellaneous: Cooking spray, almond milk, chia seeds, soy sauce.

Week 8 Prep Tips

- Batch Cook: Make lentil curry and balsamic-glazed chicken ahead of time.
- Pre-Chop Vegetables: Prepare cucumbers, carrots, and bell peppers for snacks.
- Marinate Proteins: Pre-marinate chicken for dinners.
- Prepare Overnight: Set up overnight oats and chia pudding for easy breakfasts.

Chapter 9

Incorporating Exercise for Maximum Results

Engaging in regular physical activity complements a zero-point eating plan and maximizes weight loss and overall health. Wall Pilates is an excellent form of low-impact exercise that strengthens the core, improves flexibility, and enhances muscle tone. Here are some simple Wall Pilates exercises that you can integrate into your daily routine:

Simple Wall Pilates Exercises

1. Wall Roll-Downs

- Benefits: Improves spinal flexibility and warms up the core muscles.
- How to Perform:
  1. Stand with your back against the wall, feet hip-width apart and a few inches away from the wall.
  2. Slowly roll your spine down, one vertebra at a time, until your hands reach your knees or the floor.
  3. Hold the stretch for a few seconds and then roll back up, pressing each vertebra into the wall as you go.
- Repetitions: Repeat 8-10 times.

2. Wall Leg Raises

- Benefits: Strengthens the lower abdominal muscles and improves leg flexibility.
- How to Perform:
  1. Lie on your back with your legs extended up the wall and your arms at your sides.
  2. Slowly lower one leg down the wall until you feel a stretch, then raise it back up.
  3. Alternate between legs in a controlled motion.
- Repetitions: Repeat 10-12 times per leg.

3. Wall Squats

- Benefits: Engages the quadriceps, hamstrings, and glutes while also stabilizing the core.
- How to Perform:
  1. Stand with your back against the wall and feet about two feet away from the wall.
  2. Slide down the wall until your knees form a 90-degree angle.
  3. Hold the position for 10-20 seconds, then push back up.
- Repetitions: Repeat 8-10 times.

4. Wall Planks

- Benefits: Strengthens the core, shoulders, and arms.
- How to Perform:
  1. Stand facing the wall and place your forearms on the wall, shoulder-width apart.
  2. Step back with your feet until your body forms a straight line from head to heels.
  3. Hold this position for 20-30 seconds, keeping your core tight.
  4. Repetitions: Hold for 2-3 sets.

5. Leg Press Against the Wall

- Benefits: Tones the glutes and thighs while also engaging the core.
- How to Perform:
  1. Lie on your back with your legs bent at a 90-degree angle and feet pressed against the wall.
  2. Push your feet against the wall as if you were pushing an imaginary weight.
  3. Return to the starting position.
- Repetitions: Repeat 10-15 times.

6. Wall Bridge Pose

- Benefits: Strengthens the lower back, glutes, and hamstrings.
- How to Perform:
  1. Lie on your back with your feet flat on the wall and knees bent.
  2. Lift your hips off the ground until your body forms a straight line from shoulders to knees.
  3. Hold for a few seconds, then lower back down.
- Repetitions: Repeat 8-12 times.

7. Wall Leg Circles

- Benefits: Improves hip mobility and strengthens the hip flexors and lower abs.
- How to Perform:
  1. Lie on your back with your legs extended up the wall.
  2. Move one leg in a circular motion clockwise for 5 repetitions, then switch to counterclockwise.
  3. Repeat with the other leg.
- Repetitions: Perform 5-8 circles in each direction per leg.

8. Side Leg Lifts Against the Wall

- Benefits: Tones the outer thighs and hips.
- How to Perform:
  1. Stand sideways next to the wall, using one hand for support.
  2. Lift your outer leg straight out to the side, keeping it in line with your body.
  3. Lower it back down in a controlled motion.
- Repetitions: Repeat 10-15 times per leg.

Tips for Success:

- Warm-Up First: Before starting any exercise routine, spend 5-10 minutes warming up with gentle movements such as marching in place or arm circles.
- Maintain Proper Form: Focus on slow, controlled movements to engage the right muscles and avoid strain.
- Breathe Consistently: Inhale through the nose and exhale through the mouth, ensuring that you breathe steadily during each movement.
- Listen to Your Body: If an exercise feels too intense or causes discomfort, modify it or reduce the number of repetitions.
- Combine with Daily Activity: Pair Wall Pilates exercises with daily walking or light cardio for better cardiovascular health and more comprehensive weight loss results.

Integrating these simple Wall Pilates exercises into your weekly routine will help you build strength, improve flexibility, and enhance overall fitness while complementing your zero-point meal plan for maximum results.

10-Minute Workouts to Complement Your Diet

Incorporating short, effective workouts into your day can enhance your weight loss and overall well-being. These 10-minute routines are designed to complement your zero-point eating plan and can be done at home without any equipment.

1. Full-Body Circuit Workout

- Purpose: Boost metabolism and tone the entire body.
- Routine:
  1. Jumping Jacks (1 min): Get your heart rate up and warm up your body.
  2. Bodyweight Squats (1 min): Engage your quads and glutes; keep your back straight.
  3. Push-Ups (1 min): Strengthen your chest, shoulders, and triceps. Modify by doing knee push-ups if needed.
  4. Mountain Climbers (1 min): A great cardio move that also targets your core.
  5. Wall Sit (1 min): Hold a seated position against a wall to activate your legs and core.
  6. Lunges (1 min): Alternate legs, keeping your knees aligned with your toes.

7. Plank Hold (1 min): Engage your core, keeping your body in a straight line.
8. High Knees (1 min): Raise your knees quickly, engaging your core and boosting cardio.
9. Tricep Dips (1 min): Use a sturdy chair or low table for support.
10. Cool Down with Stretching (1 min): Stretch your arms, legs, and back to prevent stiffness.

2. Core Strength Routine

- Purpose: Build core stability and strength.
- Routine:
    1. Bicycle Crunches (1 min): Lie on your back and alternate touching elbows to opposite knees.
    2. Leg Raises (1 min): Keep your legs straight and lift them to engage your lower abs.
    3. Russian Twists (1 min): Sit on the floor with your legs bent, twisting side to side.
    4. Plank Jacks (1 min): Start in a plank and jump your legs in and out.
    5. Flutter Kicks (1 min): Lie flat and flutter your legs in a quick, scissor-like motion.
    6. Side Plank (30 sec each side): Target the obliques by holding a side plank.

7. Sit-Ups (1 min): Perform controlled sit-ups to strengthen your upper abs.
8. Toe Touches (1 min): Lie on your back and reach for your toes.
9. Mountain Climbers (1 min): Speed up to engage your core and burn calories.
10. Child's Pose Stretch (1 min): Cool down with a gentle stretch for your back and core.

3. Lower Body Burn

- Purpose: Tone and strengthen legs and glutes.
- Routine:
    1. Bodyweight Squats (1 min): Engage your glutes and quads.
    2. Sumo Squats (1 min): Wider stance to target inner thighs.
    3. Lunges (1 min): Alternate legs, stepping forward and lowering into a lunge.
    4. Glute Bridges (1 min): Lie on your back, lifting your hips off the ground.
    5. Wall Sit (1 min): Hold the position to build leg strength.
    6. Calf Raises (1 min): Stand and raise onto your toes, then lower.
    7. Leg Pulses (1 min each leg): Lift one leg back and pulse to activate glutes.
    8. Side Leg Lifts (1 min): Lift your leg to the side to engage outer thighs.

9. Reverse Lunges (1 min): Step back into lunges for balance and strength.
10. Hamstring Stretch (1 min): Stretch your legs to prevent soreness.

4. Upper Body Quick Set

- Purpose: Strengthen the arms, shoulders, and chest.
- Routine:
  1. Arm Circles (1 min): Small circles forward and backward to warm up.
  2. Push-Ups (1 min): Engage chest, shoulders, and triceps. Modify to knee push-ups if needed.
  3. Tricep Dips (1 min): Use a chair to work the triceps.
  4. Shoulder Taps (1 min): In a plank position, tap each shoulder with the opposite hand.
  5. Plank Hold (1 min): Engage the core and arms.
  6. Lateral Arm Raises (1 min): Use water bottles or light weights if available.
  7. Wall Push-Ups (1 min): A modified push-up for beginners or to vary muscle engagement.
  8. Bicep Curls (1 min): Use water bottles or weights, lifting up and down.
  9. Diamond Push-Ups (1 min): Place your hands close to work the triceps more intensely.
  10. Arm Stretch (1 min): Stretch your arms to prevent tightness.

5. Cardio Boost

- Purpose: Increase heart rate and burn calories quickly.
- Routine:
  1. Jump Rope (Imaginary or with rope) (1 min): Boosts cardio and leg strength.
  2. High Knees (1 min): Drive your knees up to engage the core and legs.
  3. Burpees (1 min): Combine a squat, jump, and push-up to work the whole body.
  4. Mountain Climbers (1 min): Speed up to raise heart rate.
  5. Side-to-Side Hops (1 min): Engage legs and glutes while improving agility.
  6. Skaters (1 min): Jump side to side, mimicking a skating motion.
  7. Jumping Jacks (1 min): Engage the whole body while burning calories.
  8. Butt Kicks (1 min): Kick your heels up to engage hamstrings.
  9. Lateral Shuffles (1 min): Quick shuffles to work on speed and coordination.
  10. Cool Down with Stretching (1 min): Stretch all major muscle groups to cool down.

Tips for Success:

- Warm-Up and Cool Down: Always include a brief warm-up and cool down with each workout to prevent injury and aid recovery.

- Stay Hydrated: Drink water before and after your workout to stay hydrated.
- Modify as Needed: If an exercise feels too intense, modify it to suit your fitness level.
- Consistency is Key: Aim to complete one or two 10-minute sessions daily to see lasting results.
- Combine Workouts: Mix and match these 10-minute workouts throughout the week for variety and comprehensive fitness.

These 10-minute workouts are designed to be quick, effective, and easy to incorporate into your daily schedule, helping you build strength, improve cardio fitness, and support your weight loss goals alongside your healthy eating plan.

Stretching and Mobility Tips for All Fitness Levels

Maintaining flexibility and mobility is essential for overall fitness and helps prevent injuries. Whether you're new to exercise or an experienced athlete, these stretching and mobility tips can be easily incorporated into your daily routine to enhance your range of motion, relieve tension, and support muscle recovery.

1. Start with Dynamic Stretches for Warm-Up

- Tip: Use dynamic stretches before a workout to prepare your muscles for activity and reduce the risk of injury.

Examples:
- Leg Swings: Stand on one leg and swing the other forward and backward in a controlled motion.
- Arm Circles: Make large circular motions with your arms, both forwards and backwards, to loosen the shoulders.
- Torso Twists: Stand with feet hip-width apart and gently twist your upper body from side to side.

2. Incorporate Static Stretches After Workouts

- Tip: Use static stretching after a workout to help cool down and improve flexibility.

Examples:
- Hamstring Stretch: Sit with one leg extended and reach forward to touch your toes, holding for 15-30 seconds.
- Quad Stretch: Stand on one leg and pull the opposite foot towards your glutes, keeping your knees close together.
- Shoulder Stretch: Bring one arm across your chest and use the opposite hand to hold it in place, stretching the shoulder for 15-30 seconds.

3. Focus on Major Muscle Groups

- Tip: Target large muscle groups to ensure overall flexibility and balance.

Examples:

- Hip Flexor Stretch: Kneel on one knee and push your hips forward to stretch the front of the hip.
- Calf Stretch: Stand facing a wall, step one foot back, and press the heel down while bending the front knee.
- Back Stretch: Sit cross-legged and extend your arms forward on the floor, leaning into a gentle back stretch.

4. Use Active Isolated Stretching (AIS)

- Tip: This technique involves holding a stretch for only 2-3 seconds and repeating it 8-10 times. It promotes flexibility without causing muscle fatigue.

Examples:

- Hamstring AIS: Lie on your back and use a strap or towel to pull one leg up, holding for a few seconds before lowering it and repeating.

5. Incorporate Mobility Drills

- Tip: Add mobility exercises to increase joint flexibility and range of motion.

Examples:

- Cat-Cow Stretch: Get on all fours and alternate between arching and rounding your back to mobilize the spine.
- Ankle Circles: Sit or stand and rotate your ankle in circular motions to improve ankle flexibility.
- Thoracic Rotations: Sit on your heels, place one hand behind your head, and rotate your upper body toward the raised elbow.

6. Practice Deep Breathing During Stretches

- Tip: Deep breathing helps relax the muscles and allows for a more effective stretch.

How to Apply:

- Inhale deeply through the nose as you prepare for the stretch, and exhale slowly as you move deeper into it. This helps increase oxygen flow and relaxation.

7. Stretch Regularly for Lasting Benefits

- Tip: Consistency is key. Stretching once a week won't yield the same benefits as daily stretching.
- Recommendation: Set aside at least 10 minutes daily to focus on stretching all major muscle groups for improved flexibility over time.

8. Try Foam Rolling for Myofascial Release

- Tip: Foam rolling can relieve muscle tightness and improve mobility by targeting fascia, the connective tissue surrounding muscles.

How to Use:

- Roll gently over tight areas, like the calves or thighs, spending 1-2 minutes on each muscle group.
- Avoid rolling directly on joints or bones.

9. Engage in Yoga or Pilates

- Tip: Yoga and Pilates are excellent for enhancing flexibility, strength, and mobility.

Poses to Try:

- Downward Dog: Stretches the hamstrings, calves, and shoulders.
- Child's Pose: Stretches the back, hips, and thighs while promoting relaxation.
- Bridge Pose: Improves back flexibility and strengthens the glutes.

10. Listen to Your Body

- Tip: Stretching should not be painful. If you feel sharp or intense pain, ease out of the stretch.

- Guideline: Go to the point of mild tension, hold, and breathe deeply. Over time, you will notice an increase in your range of motion.

Additional Stretching Tips:

- Warm Muscles First: Stretching cold muscles can lead to strains. Do a light warm-up like jogging in place for 2-3 minutes before stretching.
- Hold Stretches Long Enough: For static stretches, hold each one for at least 15-30 seconds for the best effect.
- Hydrate: Proper hydration helps maintain muscle elasticity and prevents cramping.

By incorporating these stretching and mobility tips, you can enhance your overall fitness, improve your range of motion, and support muscle recovery, making your fitness journey more effective and enjoyable.

Chapter 10

Lifestyle Tips for Long-Term Success

Sustaining a healthy lifestyle requires more than just following a diet plan. It involves adopting habits that encourage long-term success and help navigate challenges. This chapter provides practical advice to stay on track, involve your family, and simplify meal prep to make your zero-point journey effective and enjoyable.

How to Stay on Track and Avoid Common Pitfalls

Staying committed to a new lifestyle can be challenging, especially when facing common obstacles. Here's how to overcome them:

1. Set Realistic Goals:
    o   Tip: Set achievable milestones that motivate you without overwhelming you.
    o   Application: Instead of aiming to lose a large amount of weight quickly, focus on smaller, consistent progress, like losing 1-2 pounds per week.
2. Track Your Progress:
    o   Tip: Use a journal or an app to log meals, workouts, and how you're feeling each day.
    o   Application: Keeping track of what you eat and how you move helps you stay accountable and see patterns in your habits.
3. Stay Flexible with Your Routine:
    o   Tip: Life happens, so be ready to adjust your plan. Flexibility helps prevent discouragement when plans change.
    o   Application: If you miss a workout or have an unplanned meal out, don't view it as a failure. Get back on track with your next meal or activity.
4. Prepare for Cravings and Social Situations:
    o   Tip: Plan ahead for social gatherings or moments when you're tempted to eat high-point foods.
    o   Application: Bring a zero-point dish to share at social events or eat a small, healthy snack beforehand to avoid overeating.
5. Find a Support System:

- Tip: Surround yourself with supportive friends, family, or online communities that encourage healthy habits.
- Application: Join a group or forum where you can share successes, struggles, and tips with others on a similar path.

6. Practice Mindful Eating:
   - Tip: Slow down and pay attention to what and how much you are eating.
   - Application: Avoid eating in front of screens and instead, focus on the taste and texture of your food, which can help you feel more satisfied.

Including the Whole Family in Your Zero Point Journey

Making lifestyle changes is more manageable when everyone in the household is on board. Here are ways to include your family:

1. Make Meals Family-Friendly:
   - Tip: Adapt zero-point recipes to suit everyone's tastes.
   - Application: Add sides like rice or pasta for family members who aren't on a zero-point diet, while you enjoy the main dish as is.

2. Get Kids Involved:
   - Tip: Engage children by letting them help with meal prep or choose which fruits and vegetables to include.
   - Application: Simple tasks like washing vegetables or setting the table make them feel involved and more likely to try new foods.

3. Plan Active Family Outings:
   - Tip: Incorporate fun activities like bike rides, hikes, or backyard games to get everyone moving.
   - Application: Schedule weekend outings that are enjoyable and promote physical activity without feeling like structured exercise.

4. Create a Meal Plan Together:
   - Tip: Let your family participate in meal planning by suggesting dishes they like.
   - Application: This ensures everyone has meals they enjoy while keeping you on track with your zero-point plan.

5. Celebrate Successes as a Family:
   - Tip: Recognize milestones and celebrate with non-food rewards like a family movie night or an outing.
   - Application: This creates a positive environment and

reinforces healthy habits for everyone.

Meal Prep Tips to Save Time and Effort

Meal prep is essential for staying consistent, reducing stress, and avoiding the temptation of quick, less healthy options. Here's how to make it easier:

1. Plan Your Week:
   o Tip: Schedule a time each week to plan your meals and create a shopping list.
   o Application: Knowing what you'll be cooking saves time during the week and helps you avoid last-minute unhealthy choices.
2. Batch Cook:
   o Tip: Prepare larger quantities of meals that can be stored and reheated throughout the week.
   o Application: Dishes like Turkey Chili with Beans or Zero Point Lentil Curry can be made in bulk and stored in individual containers.
3. Pre-Cut Ingredients:
   o Tip: Chop vegetables and portion out ingredients ahead of time to reduce prep time when cooking.

   o Application: Store pre-cut veggies in airtight containers for easy access throughout the week.
4. Use Freezer-Friendly Recipes:
   o Tip: Prepare meals that freeze well, so you always have a healthy option available.
   o Application: Soups, stews, and casseroles like Cabbage Roll Casserole can be made and frozen for future meals.
5. Organize Your Kitchen:
   o Tip: Keep your kitchen workspace organized and stocked with essentials to make meal prep smoother.
   o Application: Store frequently used items like spices, measuring tools, and storage containers within easy reach.
6. Set Up Snack Packs:
   o Tip: Portion out zero-point snacks like Spicy Roasted Chickpeas or Fresh Apple Cider Vinegar Slaw into grab-and-go containers.
   o Application: Having healthy snacks ready to eat helps avoid reaching for less nutritious options.
7. Embrace One-Pot Meals:
   o Tip: Save time on cleanup by making meals in one pot or pan.

o   Application: Recipes like Zero Point Stir-Fry with Seasonal Vegetables or Baked Lemon Herb Fish with Steamed Vegetables minimize both cooking and dishwashing time.

8. Invest in Good Storage Containers:

o   Tip: Use clear, airtight containers to keep meals fresh and make it easy to see what's inside.

o   Application: Choose containers that can go from the fridge to the microwave for added convenience.

Adopting these lifestyle tips will help you stay on track, include your loved ones in your journey, and make meal prep less of a chore. The goal is to build a sustainable, enjoyable routine that supports your zero-point diet and overall well-being.

Chapter 11

Troubleshooting and FAQs

Transitioning to a new way of eating often brings up questions and challenges. This chapter addresses some of the most common concerns and provides solutions to help you stay confident and informed on your zero-point journey.

Why Are Some Recipes Zero Points?

- Explanation: Zero-point foods are considered nutritionally dense and unlikely to be overconsumed. They include items like non-starchy vegetables, fruits, lean proteins, and certain legumes.
- Purpose: These foods encourage healthy eating habits by making it easier to build satisfying meals without worrying about point calculations.
- Application: Recipes in this book that combine zero-point ingredients remain zero points. For example, dishes like Savory Zero Point Omelet with Vegetables or Cucumber and Tomato Salad with Basil use only zero-point foods.

How Zero Points Are Calculated

- Concept: Zero-point foods are based on the Weight Watchers (WW) guidelines, where foods that are low in calories and high in nutrients earn zero points.
- Clarification: While some recipes may include minimal amounts of oil or seasonings, they're still considered zero points if they meet the criteria outlined by WW or similar point-based systems.

How to Adapt Recipes for Different Dietary Needs

Vegetarian and Vegan Options

- Tip: Replace animal proteins with plant-based alternatives like tofu, tempeh, or beans.
- Example: Swap chicken in recipes like Chicken Lettuce Wraps with marinated tofu or chickpeas for a vegan alternative.
- Dairy-Free Adaptations: Substitute dairy products with plant-based options like almond yogurt or cashew cream.

Gluten-Free Adjustments

- Tip: Substitute whole wheat pasta or bread with gluten-free versions, such as rice noodles or gluten-free bread.
- Example: Use gluten-free breadcrumbs for recipes like Zoodle Spaghetti with Turkey Meat Sauce or serve Herb-Roasted Chicken Thighs with a side of quinoa instead of whole wheat pasta.

Low-Carb Modifications

- Tip: Replace higher-carb ingredients with low-carb alternatives such as zucchini noodles, cauliflower rice, or spaghetti squash.
- Example: For a lower-carb version of Vegetable Paella, use cauliflower rice in place of traditional rice.

Nut-Free Options

- Tip: Avoid recipes that use nuts or nut-based products, or substitute with seeds like sunflower seeds or pumpkin seeds if they align with your dietary needs.
- Example: In a recipe like Simple Guacamole with Crunchy Veggies, skip any optional nuts for a nut-free version.

Common Questions Answered

Q1: Can I Meal Prep Zero Point Meals in Advance?

- Answer: Absolutely. Most zero-point meals are perfect for meal prep and can be stored in airtight containers in the refrigerator for up to 4-5 days. Dishes like Zero Point Lentil Curry and Turkey Chili with Beans freeze well for long-term storage.

Q2: Are Zero Point Foods Truly Unlimited?

- Answer: While zero-point foods can be eaten freely, it's essential to practice mindful eating. Overeating, even zero-point foods, can lead to consuming more calories than your body needs.
- Tip: Balance your plate with a variety of food groups and listen to your body's hunger cues.

Q3: How Do I Make the Recipes More Flavorful Without Adding Points?

- Answer: Use herbs, spices, and non-point seasonings like lemon juice, vinegar, garlic, ginger, and hot sauce to enhance the flavor of dishes without adding points.
- Application: Add fresh basil to Tomato Basil Gazpacho or squeeze lemon juice over Grilled Chicken

and Spinach Salad for an extra burst of flavor.

Q4: What If I Don't Have All the Ingredients for a Recipe?

- Answer: Substitute with similar zero-point or low-point ingredients.
- Example: If a recipe calls for spinach and you only have kale, feel free to use it. Missing chickpeas? Replace them with black beans in dishes like Mediterranean Chickpea Salad.

Q5: Can These Recipes Be Adapted for Family Meals?

- Answer: Yes, many of the zero-point recipes can be adapted to feed your whole family. Add sides like rice, pasta, or bread for those not following a zero-point plan, while you enjoy the zero-point main dish.
- Example: Serve Herb-Roasted Chicken Thighs with a side of mashed potatoes for the family, and have yours with a side of steamed broccoli.

Q6: How Can I Make Sure I'm Getting Enough Protein?

- Answer: Focus on zero-point lean proteins like chicken breast, fish, tofu, and eggs. Combine them with beans, legumes, and low-fat dairy for a balanced meal.

- Tip: Recipes like Grilled Zucchini Lasagna and Shrimp Stir-Fry with Snow Peas are rich in protein and zero points.

Q7: How Do I Avoid Boredom with My Meals?

- Answer: Incorporate a variety of recipes and experiment with different flavor profiles. Rotate dishes weekly and try new cooking methods like grilling, air-frying, and roasting.
- Application: Alternate between meals like Eggplant Parmesan with Tomato Sauce and Sweet Potato Shepherd's Pie to keep things interesting.

Q8: Can I Eat Out While Sticking to a Zero Point Plan?

- Answer: Yes, eating out is possible with a bit of planning. Choose dishes that align with your zero-point foods, like salads, grilled proteins, and steamed vegetables.
- Tip: Request dressings and sauces on the side and opt for dishes that are grilled, baked, or steamed rather than fried.

Q9: What Are Some Quick Snack Ideas?

- Answer: Zero-point snacks include fresh fruits, veggie sticks with Cucumber Dill Dip, or Baked Kale

Chips. These are easy to prep and satisfying.

- Application: Keep prepped snack packs of Spicy Roasted Chickpeas or Pickled Vegetables in the fridge for grab-and-go options.

Q10: How Do I Get Back on Track After a Slip-Up?

- Answer: One off-plan meal or day doesn't mean you've failed. Get back on track by resuming your regular eating pattern at your next meal.
- Tip: Reflect on why you deviated and create a plan to handle similar situations in the future, whether it's keeping healthier snacks on hand or planning ahead for social events.

These FAQs and troubleshooting tips provide practical solutions to help you stay on track, adapt to different needs, and make the most out of your zero-point journey.

Appendices

Conversion Tables and Measurement Guide

Liquid Measurements

Imperial (U.S.)	Metric
1 teaspoon (tsp)	5 milliliters (ml)
1 tablespoon (tbsp)	15 milliliters (ml)
1 fluid ounce (fl oz)	30 milliliters (ml)
1 cup	240 milliliters (ml)
1 pint (pt)	480 milliliters (ml)
1 quart (qt)	950 milliliters (ml)
1 gallon (gal)	3.8 liters (L)

Dry Measurements

Imperial (U.S.)	Metric
1/4 teaspoon	1.25 milliliters (ml)
1/2 teaspoon	2.5 milliliters (ml)
1/3 cup	80 milliliters (ml)
1/2 cup	120 milliliters (ml)
2/3 cup	160 milliliters (ml)
3/4 cup	180 milliliters (ml)
1 cup	120 grams (g) flour*
1 cup	200 grams (g) sugar*

*Note: Weight varies based on the type of ingredient. Use specific ingredient weights for greater accuracy.

Weight Conversions

Imperial (U.S.)	Metric
1 ounce (oz)	28 grams (g)
8 ounces	227 grams (g)
1 pound (lb)	454 grams (g)
2.2 pounds (lb)	1 kilogram (kg)

Quick Reference for Temperature Conversions

Celsius (°C)	Fahrenheit (°F)
100°C	212°F (boiling point of water)
200°C	392°F
180°C	356°F
160°C	320°F
150°C	302°F
120°C	248°F
0°C	32°F (freezing point of water)

Tip: To convert °C to °F, use the formula:
$$°F = (°C × 9/5) + 32$$

To convert °F to °C, use the formula:
$$°C = (°F − 32) × 5/9$$

Common Ingredient Weights and Equivalents

Flour (All-Purpose)

Measurement	Weight (grams)
1 cup	120 g
1/2 cup	60 g
1/3 cup	40 g
1/4 cup	30 g

Sugar (Granulated)

Measurement	Weight (grams)
1 cup	200 g
1/2 cup	100 g
1/3 cup	65 g
1/4 cup	50 g

Butter

Measurement	Weight (grams)
1 cup	227 g (2 sticks)
1/2 cup	113 g (1 stick)
1/4 cup	57 g
1 tbsp	14 g

Useful Kitchen Measurement Tips

1. Leveling Dry Ingredients: Use a knife or flat spatula to level off dry ingredients like flour and sugar for accurate measurement.
2. Liquids at Eye Level: When measuring liquids, check the measurement at eye level to ensure precision.
3. Converting Recipes: To scale a recipe up or down, double or halve each ingredient while maintaining the same ratios.
4. Weight vs. Volume: Measuring by weight is generally more accurate for baking, especially for flour and dry ingredients.

This conversion table and guide are designed to help you confidently tackle any recipe, no matter its origin. Keep these references handy as you explore new dishes and continue your journey toward delicious and healthy zero-point cooking.

Index

Recommended Resources for Further Reading

Books

1. "The Blue Zones Kitchen: 100 Recipes to Live to 100" by Dan Buettner
   o A cookbook inspired by regions with the highest life expectancy, focusing on whole, plant-based foods that promote longevity.
2. "The Obesity Code: Unlocking the Secrets of Weight Loss" by Dr. Jason Fung
   o A comprehensive look at the science behind weight gain and how intermittent fasting and balanced nutrition can help you manage weight.
3. "Eat to Live" by Dr. Joel Fuhrman
   o This book offers a nutrient-dense, plant-based diet plan designed to help you lose weight and improve your overall health.
4. "How Not to Diet: The Groundbreaking Science of Healthy, Permanent Weight Loss" by Dr. Michael Greger
   o An evidence-based guide focusing on diet strategies proven to aid in weight loss without restrictive dieting.
5. "The Complete Mediterranean Cookbook" by America's Test Kitchen
   o Packed with over 500 recipes, this book emphasizes the benefits of the Mediterranean diet, known for its heart-healthy and weight management qualities.

Websites

1. Weight Watchers (WW) Official Site (www.weightwatchers.com)
   o Offers resources on zero-point foods, meal planning, and lifestyle tips aligned with the WW system.
2. MyFitnessPal (www.myfitnesspal.com)
   o A free app and website that helps you track meals, exercise, and water intake for a comprehensive view of your wellness journey.
3. EatRight.org (Academy of Nutrition and Dietetics)
   o Features articles and resources on nutrition, healthy recipes, and wellness tips from registered dietitians.
4. Forks Over Knives (www.forksoverknives.com)
   o Focuses on the benefits of a whole-food, plant-based diet with recipes, articles, and cooking tips.
5. The Spruce Eats (www.thespruceeats.com)

- Provides a wide array of healthy recipes and cooking guides that cater to different dietary needs and preferences.

Tools and Apps

1. WW App
   - An excellent companion for those following the Weight Watchers program, offering easy tracking, recipes, and community support.
2. MyPlate by Livestrong
   - A user-friendly app that helps you track your daily intake, set weight goals, and monitor nutritional habits.
3. Cronometer
   - A comprehensive tool for tracking calories, nutrients, and macros, making it easy to ensure balanced nutrition.
4. FitOn App
   - Offers free, guided workouts ranging from Pilates and yoga to HIIT, which pair well with your zero-point meal plan for an overall fitness boost.

Podcasts

1. "The Nutrition Diva's Quick and Dirty Tips for Eating Well and Feeling Fabulous"
   - A podcast that offers practical, evidence-based tips on healthy eating and nutrition in short, digestible episodes.
2. "Food Psych Podcast with Christy Harrison"
   - Explores topics related to intuitive eating, body positivity, and breaking the diet culture for sustainable weight management.
3. "The Doctor's Farmacy with Mark Hyman, M.D."
   - Covers various topics on health, nutrition, and wellness, often featuring expert interviews and actionable advice.

Online Courses

1. "Plant-Based Nutrition" by eCornell
   - A certificate program designed to educate participants on the benefits of plant-based eating and how it can improve health.
2. "Nutrition and Healthy Living" by edX
   - Offers a comprehensive look at the basics of nutrition, healthy eating habits, and the science behind different diet plans.

3. "Weight Management: Beyond Balancing Calories" by Coursera
    o A course that dives into factors affecting weight management, including metabolism, behavioral strategies, and nutritional science.

Professional Support

- Registered Dietitians (RDs) and Nutritionists
    o Consulting with a registered dietitian can provide tailored guidance and personalized meal plans that align with your health goals.
- Health Coaches
    o Working with a health coach can offer motivation, accountability, and tips on integrating new habits into your routine.

Thank You

Dear Reader,

Thank you for choosing *Super Easy Zero Point Weight Loss Cookbook*. I truly hope this book has provided you with practical tools, delicious recipes, and helpful insights to support your weight loss and healthy living journey. Your dedication and commitment to making positive lifestyle changes inspire me, and it has been an honor to be a part of your path to wellness.

If you found value in this book, I would greatly appreciate it if you could take a moment to leave a review. Your feedback helps others discover the benefits of zero-point eating and supports me in creating more resources that serve your needs.

Thank you once again for your trust and support. Wishing you continued success on your health journey!

Warmest regards,
Fiona Westbrook

Made in the USA
Coppell, TX
24 November 2024

40943030R00070